SECRET BUFFALO

A Guide to the Weird, Wonderful, and Obscure

Elizabeth Licata

Reedy Press
PO Box 5131
St. Louis, MO 63139
www.reedypress.com

Library of Congress Control Number: 2019952743
ISBN: 9781681062594

Design by Jill Halpin

Cover images: Sunflower by Elizabeth Licata, shed by kc kratt photography, ceiling by J. P. Thimot, shark girl by Elizabeth Licata, Headshot by kc kratt photography

All images are courtesy of the author unless otherwise noted.

Printed in the United States of America
21 22 23 24 25   5 4 3 2

This book is dedicated with thanks
to my husband, Alan Bigelow.

Photo by Elizabeth Licata

CONTENTS

Photo by Stephen Gabris

ACKNOWLEDGMENTS

Much of the information in this book is drawn from more than 20 years of experience as editor of *Buffalo Spree* magazine, where I am always looking for interesting experiences to share with our Western New York readership. Some local websites that I explore regularly for this purpose include Visit Buffalo Niagara (visitbuffaloniagara.com), Western New York's excellent convention and visitor's bureau; Buffalo Rising (buffalorising.com), a longtime online source of local info; the *Buffalo News* (buffalonews.com), our daily paper; and Chuck LaChiusa's Buffalo Architecture and History (buffaloah.com).

Some books that were particularly helpful include *Buffalo Everything: A Guide to Eating in the "Nickel City,"* by Arthur Bovino, which is, by far, the most comprehensive and well-researched guide to Buffalo's food scene; the many Images of America books that focus on Western New York; and Christine A. Smyczynski's guides to the area, including *Explorer's Guide: Buffalo & Niagara Falls*. I also salute Bruce Kershner's *Secret Places: Scenic Treasures of Western New York*, which is out of print but is being revived by authors Jennifer Hillman and Bill McKeever.

I must also acknowledge the excellent work of kc kratt photography which supplied many of the images used in this book. In almost every case, these images were originally shot for *Buffalo Spree*.

Photo by Elizabeth Licata

INTRODUCTION

There's a building at 812 Main St. that's emblazoned with the words, KEEP BUFFALO A SECRET, in five-foot-high letters. It's a highly visible admission that, in Buffalo, everything is considered a secret. For decades, Buffalonians have assumed, rightly, that most outsiders know very little about their city except that Buffalo found a way to give America chicken wings despite being buried in snow most of the time. Those assumptions have changed over the past 20 years. Buffalo's amazing natural assets, cultural treasures, architectural riches, and edible delights are being discovered by new residents and visitors alike. It still makes the question of what is well known and lesser known difficult to parse.

Some things here, such as the Dnipro Ukrainian Cultural Center, have been part of the daily lives of some Buffalonians for many years, but still are unknown outside their neighborhoods. There are new additions, such as Oxford Pennant, that all the cool kids know about, but that would be completely unfamiliar to the other 80 percent. And there are a few items that almost nobody knows about, such as the thwarted Jewish homeland on Grand Island and the lonely Metcalfe House remnants in Buffalo State College's Rockwell Hall.

The fact that Buffalo has a huge mural screaming about its secrecy is testimony to the city's sense of humor as well as its pride. The very idea of secrecy is built on shifting sands in Buffalo. The items in this book, regardless of their levels of secrecy, are presented to help readers understand why Buffalonians love their city and why some of them may really wish to keep it a secret—sometimes.

ART UNDERGROUND

Where is the most underappreciated civic project in Buffalo?

In 1986, Buffalo finished its first subway line. With a straight shot down Main Street from the University at Buffalo's city campus to the KeyBank center downtown, the line includes just 14 stops, six above ground and eight below. Yearly ridership is steady in the five to six million area, but many Buffalonians complain that it doesn't access the suburbs or the airport.

Few celebrate what Metro Rail does have: a thoughtfully curated and comprehensive public art component. There are surface and underground art installations at the seven stations large enough to accommodate them, and they often pop up in unexpected places—a key component of good public art.

Riders on the up escalator at the Amherst Street Station are treated to a hammered aluminum sculpture that was shaped by being wrapped around a tree. This work by Robert Lobe is suspended in the air above them.

Those waiting on the underground platform at Utica can ponder the meaning of four mysterious torsos, looming from structural pillars, just above head height: "The Listener" (with birds), "The Stagehand" (weights and masks), "The Choreographer-Seneca Man" (animal persona), and "The Portrait Maker" (with mirror that reflects viewers). The bronze, steel, and aluminum works are by Craig Langager.

SUBWAY ART

WHAT: An ambitious juried project that filled Buffalo subway stations with art

WHERE: Metro Rail stations from University to Allen/ Medical Campus

COST: Technically free, but to get to all the stations, it's good to buy a Metro ticket.

PRO TIP: Check buffaloah.org/a/metro/tc.html for information; for tours, check explorebuffalo.org, or just take the subway for $2.

Mosaic by Joyce Kozloff. Photo by Jean-Pierre Thimot

At Humboldt-Hospital Station, underground walkers pass by a series of photographic portraits of Buffalo steelworkers by the late Milton Rogovin, who celebrated these ordinary folks by creating extraordinary images of them at the mill and at home with their families.

Gorgeous cut glass mosaics by Joyce Kozloff are another showstopper at Humboldt-Hospital; the colorful work can also be enjoyed by passersby through the station windows.

All told, 22 artworks are positioned outside and inside these eight stations. It took more than 30 years for someone to think of offering regular tours of this project; Explore Buffalo (explorebuffalo.org) now offers them every spring and summer.

Internationally known artists were recruited to enhance Buffalo's Metro Rail experience, but busy commuters rarely take a look.

THE HOUSE THAT A PROPHECY BUILT

Think you've seen over-the-top house decorations?

Isaiah Henry Robertson, a contractor living in Niagara Falls, was visited by a divine prophecy sometime in the early 2000s. God instructed him that, come the end of the world in 2014 (oops), all of humanity would come flying by Robertson's house and that the house must become a beacon of salvation. After flying by the house and choosing salvation (or not), the multitudes would proceed to Goat Island, near Niagara Falls, where they would proceed on their upwards or downwards paths.

PROPHET ISAIAH SECOND COMING HOUSE

WHAT: It can't be described.

WHERE: 1308 Ontario St., Niagara Falls, NY

COST: Free

PRO TIP: This is a drive-by.

Prophet Isaiah's Second Coming House is the eye-popping result of this prophecy. It is a gorgeous, traffic-stopping sanctuary of colorful iconography in the middle of a drab Niagara Falls neighborhood: a beacon, indeed.

Robertson updated and refreshed the painted decorations on this property on a continual

---

It's off the beaten track, but this house is one of a few top sites missed by Niagara Falls visitors, who tend to head straight to the waterfall and then depart.

The house has been updated and further embellished over the years. Photo by kc kratt photography

basis. He also welcomed sightseers cordially, offering salvation to many of them, despite the expiration date of his original prophecy.

Isaiah Robertson passed away on January 25, 2020. According to TripAdvisor, "Prophet Isaiah's Second Coming House" ranks No. 36 among the 112 things to do in Niagara Falls. It is not clear what the upkeep plan is for this remarkable structure, so visitors are advised to see the house sooner rather than later.

PRICELESS LIBRARY TREASURES

Who has the rarest books of all?

Shakespeare's *First Folio*? Check. Original *Adventures of Huckleberry Finn* manuscript? Check. Isaac Newton's *Principia*? Check. A leaf from the *Gutenberg Bible*? Yes, the Buffalo and Erie County Public Library has that, too, as well as many, many other seminal editions of the printed word.

The *Huckleberry Finn* manuscript is part of a permanent Mark Twain exhibit, while an astounding collection of first and early editions of other famous publications is known collectively as Milestones of Science.

Milestones of Science consists of 196 titles collected by Buffalo industrialist Chauncey Hamlin in the 1930s; Depression-era prices allowed him to assemble it within a few years. The titles include first editions of works by such figures as Aristotle, Euclid, Archimedes, Copernicus, and Galileo.

The overriding concept is that each work announces groundbreaking discoveries. Even better, various Buffalo-based ethnic communities—Polish, German, Swiss, French, British, and others—contributed funds so that Hamlin could acquire the works of their countrymen. This is how internationally famous rare titles that would now be well beyond the means of any institutional budget are on view for free in downtown Buffalo.

RARE BOOKS COLLECTION

WHAT: An astounding collection of the world's most treasured books

WHERE: Downtown branch of the Buffalo and Erie County Public Library, 1 Lafayette Sq.

COST: Free

PRO TIP: These books are on display on a rotating basis, so you shouldn't expect access to all of them.

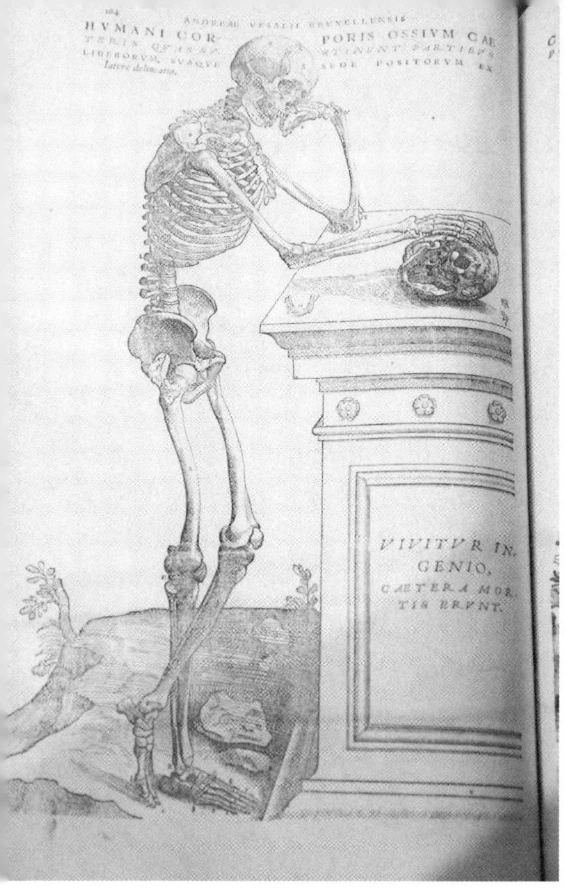

HVMANI CORPORIS OSSIVM

VIVITVR INGENIO, CÆTERA MORTIS ERVNT.

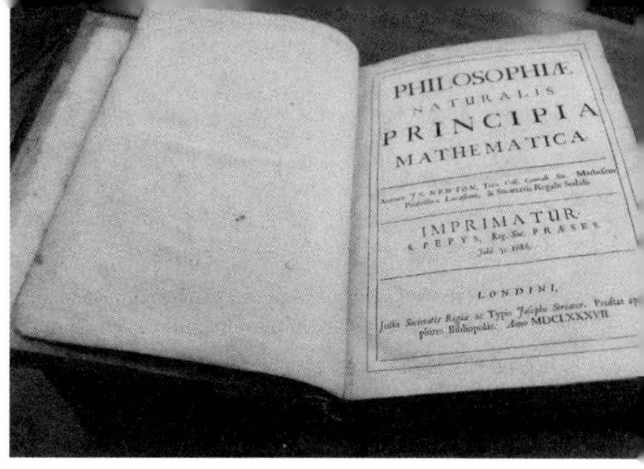

PHILOSOPHIÆ NATURALIS PRINCIPIA MATHEMATICA

IMPRIMATUR

LONDINI

MDCLXXXVII.

Above: The title page of a book on astronomy by Isaac Newton. Left: A page from Andreas Vesalius' De humani corporis fabrica. Photos by kc kratt photography

Among the other titles in this amazing collection: Galileo's *Dialogo dei Massimi Sistemi*, 1632; René Descartes's *Discours de la Méthode*, 1637; Ben Franklin's *Experiments and Observations on Electricity*, 1769; German physician and botanist Leonhart Fuchs's *De Historia Stirparum*, a catalog of medicinal plants, 1542; Robert Boyle's *The Skeptical Chymist*, 1661; Carolus Linnaeus's *Species Plantarum*, 1753; and many others.

The authors also include Johannes Kepler, Isaac Newton, Jakob Bernoulli, Andreas Vesalius, Gregor Mendel, Dmitri Mendeleyev, Madame Curie, Georges Cuvier, and Anton Van Leeuwenhoek.

The "Milestones of Science" were about to be sold by Buffalo's cash-poor Museum of Science in 1996, but it made a win/win deal with the Buffalo and Erie County Public Library to keep them in Buffalo.

AN OLD-SCHOOL IMAX

Wondering what went on in here?

Entertainment was different in the 1880s. There were no movie houses, but larger-than-life spectacles were important and were provided, either live or in the form of gigantic images. This was the concept behind cycloramas.

Cycloramas were large, circular paintings that surrounded viewers and created an illusion of being within the event depicted. And Buffalo's own Cyclorama Building was constructed in 1888 to display *The Crucifixion of Christ*, which was 360 feet long and 50 feet high. This was on view for two years, attracting as many as 1,000 visitors per day. An article at the time wrote, "The cyclorama of Jerusalem attracted crowds of people last week. The gay laughter is hushed and the smile fades from the face of the most worldly spectator when gazing at this wonderful representation which seems to bring the days of the great tragedy terribly near."

CYCLORAMA

WHAT: An unusual circular building made for spectacular experiences

WHERE: 369 Franklin St.

COST: Free

PRO TIP: Combine this with a tour of St. Louis Church, next door.

Next up was *The Battle of Gettysburg*, which was up for another two years. Unfortunately, by this time, cycloramas were no longer popular, and the circular structure was used for a variety of other

The cyclorama was built for a use that became obsolete within a decade; its survival is a testament to local preservationists.

Cycloramas were 16-sided buildings originally constructed to house panoramic art displays popular in the United States in the late 1800s. The Buffalo cyclorama is one of the few surviving cycloramas. Above: The cyclorama today. Photo by Elizabeth Licata. Inset: Interior images from the early 1900s. Photo courtesy of Library of Congress

purposes, often remaining empty—and threatened with demolition—for years at a time.

Stability came in the 1980s, when it was developed as an office building, which it remains—successfully—today. The interior shows little signs of the building's former purpose, but the exterior, though windows have been added, is still an architectural curiosity.

SECOND LIFE FOR A DEMOLISHED LANDMARK

Want to see a classic example of making the best of a bad hand?

In 1882, shortly after he joined the avant-garde architectural firm of McKim, Mead & White, Stanford White designed the James F. Metcalfe House, a large, shingle-style villa at 125 North St. This area of Buffalo is known for its mansions, many designed by well-known architects, but some did not survive the 20th century, including the Metcalfe House, which was demolished in 1980 to provide parking for the owners of the large Williams-Butler mansion next door, also designed by Stanford White.

White was known for designing lavish interiors for his houses, and three interior elements of the Metcalfe House were saved from the demolition: the library, dining room, and staircase. The staircase is in the Metropolitan Museum of Art; the dining room and library have been reconstructed inside Buffalo State College's Rockwell Hall, where they can be visited when classes are in session by contacting

METCALFE ROOMS

WHAT: Reconstructed rooms from a demolished landmark

WHERE: 122 Rockwell Hall, Buffalo State College, 1300 Elmwood Ave.

COST: Free

PRO TIP: To see these rooms, contact the Dean's Office, 122 Rockwell Hall, Buffalo State College; 716-878-6326.

These exquisite examples of Stanford White's interior design were (barely) saved from the wrecking ball.

The Metcalfe House dining room and (behind it) library. Photo by Stephen Gabris

the Dean of Students office. White's elegant ornamental woodwork makes these reconstructions well worth viewing.

Sadly, the purpose of the Metcalfe House's demolition was to make room for a parking lot that was never built. It was requested by the Delware North food service and hospitality company, which also owns the Williams-Butler Mansion adjacent to the MetCalfe House.

The reconstruction work of the rooms was financed through private donations, including $40,000 from Delaware North, and a large contribution from the Seymour H. Knox Foundation. The restored rooms opened at Buffalo State College in 1989.

SPOOKY MAGNIFICENCE IN PERRYSBURG

Just what is this doing in the middle of a forest?

About an hour southeast of downtown Buffalo, an abandoned hospital complex presents an unexpected vista of decayed magnificence surrounded by forest. The J. N. Adam Memorial Hospital was built by Buffalo mayor James Noble Adam—who also owned an eponymous department store—in 1912. The 300-acre, multibuilding campus was designed to provide the best treatment possible for tuberculosis patients. In the 1920s, tuberculosis was an acute problem through the US, and the most advanced (pre-antibiotic) treatments involved "sun therapy" and fresh air, as recommended by Swiss doctor Auguste Rollier. Architect John Coxhead did his best to provide this in his neoclassic structure by including extensive sleeping porches.

The large administration building sprawls in a semicircle and includes four patient wards and a dining hall; there are also several outbuildings. The 120,000-square-foot hospital was built on a grand scale, with

J. N. ADAM HOSPITAL

WHAT: A decaying, but still magnificent, hospital complex

WHERE: Peck Hill Rd., Perrysburg, NY

COST: Free

PRO TIP: Only the exterior can be seen without special permission.

Because of the enormous expense of doing anything, including demolition, with this property, it sits and decays.

The domed dining area and the exterior, showing some of the sleeping porches. Photos by Char Szabo-Perricelli

lofty ceilings, ornate staircases, tall columns inside and out, and, notably, a stained glass dome over the circular dining area. It was used as a tuberculosis sanitarium until 1960, when it became a state facility for the developmentally disabled. In 1991, this use ended, and the complex has been empty ever since. Devotees of ruin porn are frequent visitors, so much so that the campus has been enclosed with chain-link fencing to discourage trespassing. It still can be viewed from outside this fencing, and the drive from Buffalo is scenic, as is the campus's wooded surroundings.

A VISIT TO AN OLD FLAME

Have you undergone this local rite of passage?

Though Chestnut Ridge Park's Eternal Flame and Eternal Flame Falls are known to many Buffalonians, they exist within a secluded gorge and at the end of a moderate-to-difficult hike. As a result, casual visitors to Buffalo have likely never seen one of the region's most famous beauty sites.

Chestnut Ridge Park, established in 1926 and developed by the Works Progress Administration (WPA) in the 1930s, is located in the Buffalo suburb of Orchard Park. It's a popular spot for sledding, tobogganing, and other winter sports, as well as for family picnics, hiking, and biking in the warmer months. The park was named for its many chestnut trees, sadly wiped out, along with billions of other American chestnut trees, in a mid-century blight. Red oak and hemlock are now the dominant species in the park.

Though somewhat a rite of passage for locals, the hike to the Eternal Flame is not widely known. It starts at the Shale Creek park entrance; a wooded trail crosses Shale Creek and leads upward to the edge of a gorge, where the thundering, 35-foot waterfall and (at night) the natural gas flame at the bottom can be seen. The trail then leads downhill along the side of the ravine—keep left—and then follows the creek upstream until the Eternal Flame, at the bottom of the falls, is reached. There might be as many as three natural gas jets flaring up behind the waterfall. If they're not flaring, a barbecue lighter flicked along the back edge of the grotto will set them alight. The wet grotto rocks present more of a hazard than the mild gas flame.

Chestnut Ridge Park is gorgeous and filled with amenities; this mysterious hike is the cherry on top.

The natural gas flame can be reached after a brief hike of moderate difficulty. Photo by kc kratt photography

ETERNAL FLAME

WHAT: An eerie destination in a beautiful park

WHERE: Free

COST: 6121 Chestnut Ridge Rd., Orchard Park, NY

PRO TIP: The waterfall can be almost dry in summer; try this in spring or fall.

For those who want real drama, take this hike during the day first, for familiarization, and then again, at night, to see the flames at their best. This hike is only about a half-mile each way, but hikers will encounter hills, tree roots, wet rocks, and other obstacles. Midsummer might seem an attractive time to do this hike, but there's a chance the waterfall will be disappointing, so think of fall or spring.

A DREAM OF A WESTERN NEW YORK JEWISH HOMELAND

What was this guy thinking?

In 1824, an early American Zionist named Mordecai Manuel Noah arranged the purchase of one fifth of Grand Island, about 12 miles north of Buffalo, to be used as a Jewish homeland. The New York City–based writer talked a friend, Samuel Leggett, into financing the purchase.

In 1825, Noah traveled to Buffalo to dedicate the land, which he named Ararat. The dedication took place in St. Paul's Episcopal Cathedral, as there were not enough boats to take attendees of the dedication over to Grand Island itself. Noah declared himself "Governor and Judge of Israel" and went back to New York, leaving no one behind him to carry out his mission. There were no Jewish settlers in the Buffalo of that time, and the Eastern European Jews for whom this homeland was designated never learned of its existence.

ARARAT MARKER

WHAT: Strange remnant of a quixotic mission

WHERE: Roadside marker on Grand Island on East River Road, across from Whitehaven Cemetery; cornerstone in the Buffalo History Museum

COST: Free for the marker, admission for the cornerstone

PRO TIP: This is not easy to spot; be persistent. There are no tours.

It's unsurprising that nothing came of Noah's homeland idea, as he didn't bother to notify the people he thought could settle in it.

This roadside marker on Grand Island isn't easy to find. Photo by kc kratt photography

A stone intended to mark the site was left in St. Paul's churchyard until General Peter Porter brought it over to Grand Island, building an obelisk-shaped niche for it that could be seen from the river. It was moved several times over the decades, even returning to Buffalo at one point, when it was taken in by the Buffalo and Erie County Historical Society (now the Buffalo History Museum). The cornerstone remains in the collection of the museum.

The idea of a Jewish homeland on Grand Island may sound outlandish today, but, in the early 19th century, the terminus to the Erie Canal was not far away, and Grand Island was located between two peaceful countries.

UNDERGROUND RAILROAD HISTORY IN WESTERN NEW YORK

What's real and what's urban myth?

Buffalo and Niagara Falls, both located along the Niagara River, with Canada on the other side, played major roles in the Underground Railroad, the nationwide network of escape routes and safe houses that were used by enslaved African Americans to escape into free states and Canada. A separate book would be needed to do justice to this important part of history, but it can be summarized selectively here, with key locations available for visitation.

Buffalo

One of the most well-known abolitionists of the era, William Wells Brown, who lived in Buffalo c. 1836–45, has given firsthand accounts of fugitives he housed and helped transport to freedom. Though New York was a free state, still there was danger of fugitives being recaptured, hence the journey to Canada. Buffalo History Museum librarian Cynthia Van Ness has done extensive research on the facts and myths surrounding Underground Railroad activity in Buffalo and

UNDERGROUND RAILROAD HERITAGE CENTER

WHAT: The best place to learn about the Underground Railroad in Western New York

WHERE: 825 Depot Center W., Niagara Falls, NY

COST: Adult admission is $10; student, senior, family, and group rates are also available.

PRO TIP: Visit the Heritage Center for the most well-documented history; google to find other sites that may or may not be authentic but are still interesting.

offers first-person narratives of escapees as the most reliable evidence, as with this Brown retelling of an escapee's account:

"We reached Buffalo at 4 p.m. The captain said, that if there was any danger in the town, he would take us in his yawl and put us across. He walked through the town to see if there were any bills up. Finding no danger, he took us out of the hatchway—he walked with us as far as Black Rock Ferry, giving us good advice all the way, how we should conduct ourselves through life in Canada, and we have never departed from his directions—his counsel was good, and I have kept it."

Another story of freedom reached via the Black Rock Ferry is related by African American abolitionist and writer Samuel Ringgold Ward, who tells of a fugitive pursued right up to the boat by a former owner with a loaded pistol.

"The Negro, on the other hand, watched every inch of progress which widened the distance betwixt the two shores, until, not waiting for the boat to touch, he ran back to the stern, and then, with a full bound like a nimble deer, sprang from the boat to the shore in advance of the boat, and, rising, took off his poor old hat, and gave three cheers for the British sovereign."

The Black Rock Ferry site mentioned here is one the few that still can be visited, at the foot of Ferry Street, in Broderick Park. This is one of the few physical sites still in existence, as many of the pre-Civil War era houses of prominent Buffalo abolitionists and others who would have sheltered and helped fugitives reach freedom have been demolished over the years. In addition, Buffalo was a relatively small municipality during the pre-Civil War years, and it wouldn't have been easy to conceal strangers for very

---

Continued research remains to be done regarding the true activities of the Underground Railroad in Buffalo; some think much of what people believe is little more than wishful thinking.

long. Many historians have concluded that Buffalo was a crucial transfer point for escapees, but much more research is needed.

Niagara Falls

Exciting stories of Harriet Tubman guiding fugitives to freedom across Niagara Falls' Whirlpool Bridge have been in circulation for decades, but, thanks to a new resource, the newly opened Niagara Falls Underground Railroad Heritage Center, the truth of Niagara Falls' role in these escapes is finally brought to life with historical accuracy. Here, visitors can learn about the Cataract House, a hotel that gave employment and other help to many escapees, as well as the ferry at the base of the American Falls that was maintained by Cataract House owners. There are many great stories of Cataract House escapes, including this one from Nancy Berry, a maid who was brought to Niagara Falls by her honeymooning owners, and who took her first opportunity to flee:

"In the morning, Mr. and Mrs. Cox went for a drive, telling me that I could have the day to do as I pleased. The shores of Canada had been tantalizing my longing gaze for some days, and I was bound to reach there long before my mistress returned. So, I locked up Mrs. Cox's trunk and put the key under the pillow, where I was sure she would find it, and I made a strike for freedom! A servant in the hotel gave me all necessary information and even assisted me in getting away. Some kind of a festival was going on, and a large crowd was marching from the rink to the river, headed by a band of music. In such a motley throng I was unnoticed, but was trembling with fear of being detected. It seemed an age before the ferry boat arrived, which at last appeared, enveloped in a gigantic wreath of black smoke. Hastily I embarked, and, as the boat stole away into the misty twilight and among crushing fields of ice, though the air was chill and gloomy, I felt the warmth of freedom as I neared the Canada shore."

At the Heritage Center, the story of how prominent Niagara Falls businesspeople and African American residents worked for the freedom of others is well-told. Opened in 2018, the center is

The Heritage Center is part of a restored US Customs House; it is filled with illustrated historic narratives. Photos by Stephen Gabris

located in the restored US Custom House, built in 1863 to handle commercial traffic between the US and Canada. It fell out of this use in the 1960s, eventually being purchased by the city of Niagara Falls to be renovated as a train station, headquarters for US Customs and Border Protection, and the Heritage Center.

BUFFALO'S BARBARY COAST

How bad does a street need to be to be called Wickedest Street in the World?

Nineteenth-century waterfront life—anywhere—was not known for its decorum, and Buffalo's waterfront in the early days of the Erie Canal was notorious for its lawlessness. The area bordering today's popular, family-friendly Canalside attractions then was known as "The Infected District," and "the Wickedest Street in the World," by the journalists of the day. Canal Street was the center of the action, with 93 saloons, 100 gambling halls, 75 brothels, and 15 dance halls along both sides of Canal Street and on the small alleys and lanes connected to it. It covered the area that today includes Marine Drive Apartments, the Buffalo & Erie County Naval & Military Park, and the Liberty Hound Restaurant.

Visitors to today's Canalside are treading the same ground as the lakemen and canallers who drank and brawled in places such as Dug's Dive, called a dive because it was located below the street, at the level of the Erie Canal towpath. An 1874 *Buffalo Express* report describes it:

"The room was small, close, and ill-smelling. . . . Around the walls, benches were placed, and on these couches, the regular and transient boarders recline and sleep over their drunken stupors."

Dug's Dive was one of the few saloons where black patrons and white patrons mingled, and it served as a place to make Underground Railroad connections. A combination of the Erie Canal's premature decline as a shipping artery, modernization,

---

Buffalo's waterfront is unrecognizable from its early days, when industry, not recreation, was the goal.

Buffalo's downtown waterfront was a busy and dangerous place in the early 1800s. Photo courtesy of the Buffalo History Museum

INFECTED DISTRICT

WHAT: An early waterfront location for dens of iniquity

WHERE: Canalside, 44 Prime St.

COST: Free

PRO TIP: Try to get a copy of the out-of-print *America's Crossroads: Buffalo's Canal Street/Dante Place*, by Mike Vogel, which fully documents this history.

and public concern caused the decline of the Infected District. The canal terminus was moved north and the old canal paved over; by 1910, the area was home to Italian immigrants. In 1940, their tenements had been razed, so that the Memorial Auditorium (now demolished) could be built. The approximate location of Dug's can be viewed today, where a contemporary replica of the Whipple Truss Bridge spans the rewatered Commercial Slip at Canalside.

FROM PERILOUS SHANTYTOWN TO PEACEFUL PRESERVE

Ever heard the expression, "Nature bats last"?

A spit of land just south of downtown Buffalo, between Lake Erie and the Buffalo River, has a fascinating history. The area we now call Times Beach was formed by the same glacial advances and retreats that created the Niagara River and Falls, forming part of a rich network of marshes, deltas, sandbars, mudflats, and beaches that stretched along a long coastline. Signs of human habitation go back thousands of years, and the area would certainly have been used by Western New York's indigenous peoples for hunting, campsites, and fishing, at least in the summer months.

Europeans arrived in the 18th century, and development began in earnest with the building of the Buffalo harbor in the early 19th century. By the 1870s, a community of Irish waterfront workers had built a shantytown called Seawall Beach, where they endured harsh winter storm surges and general poverty.

In the 1920s, the shantytown was removed so that a railway could be built. There was a public beach here very briefly in 1935; thereafter, the area was used for dredging. In the 1970s, all this human activity stopped, and nature took over. Millions of migrating

TIMES BEACH

WHAT: An urban wildlife preserve

WHERE: North end of Fuhrmann Boulevard, near the Coast Guard Station

COST: Free

PRO TIP: Storms can cause closures of this site, so check before you go. Dogs are not allowed.

Wildflowers and wildlife at Times Beach. Photos by Elizabeth Licata

birds, butterflies (including the iconic Monarch butterfly), native bees and breeding birds, reptiles, mammals, and more than 100 species of native pollinators moved in.

Today, just as it did thousands of years ago, Times Beach shelters wildlife on 55 acres of undeveloped shoreline.

Monarch butterflies, red-winged blackbirds, yellow warblers, tree swallows, and American pipits are just some of the wildlife species to see here.

STONES OF A LITTLE-KNOWN HISTORY

What happened to this community?

A rusted, wrought iron arch rises over the dilapidated gates of this East Side cemetery, many of its stones covered in faded Hebrew inscriptions.

Founded in 1882, it served the congregation of the Beth Jacob synagogue, which was demolished at some point in the mid-20th century. The cemetery, now under the care of the Jewish Federation Cemetery Corporation, is one of a few remnants of a once-vibrant East Side Jewish community. The orthodox synagogue was founded by prominent East Siders Jacob H. Mayerberg (after whom the congregation was named), Louis Rubenstein, Joseph Saperston, David Friedlander, Simon Harris, and Simon Cohen. People were buried in the cemetery, located at Lansdale Street, near Doat Street, as recently as the 1980s. The Jewish Federation is seeking funds to repair and maintain the stones, fencing, lighting, and grounds.

BETH JACOB CEMETERY

WHAT: Buffalo's first Jewish cemetery

WHERE: End of Lansdale Street

COST: Free

PRO TIP: Combine this with a tour of other East Side landmarks, such as the Central Terminal.

Thanks to an Eagle Scout project and the vigilance of volunteers, the Beth Jacob Cemetery is getting more of the upkeep it deserves.

The iron arch and grave stones from the 1882 cemetery. Photos by kc kratt photography

In 2008, the *Buffalo News* noted that Congregation Beth Jacob, which no longer stands, was transferred to the Buffalo Municipal Housing Authority in May 1959 for a massive urban-renewal project. Urban renewal would contribute to the Jewish population's exodus into the suburbs and the abandonment of the city's synagogues.

Most buried in Beth Jacob Cemetery, also known as Doat Street Cemetery, died in the late 19th or early 20th centuries, with a smattering buried as late as the 1970s and 1980s, and one person in the early 1990s. Jewish Federation Cemetery Corporation assumed ownership in 2002 and ensures that the grass is mowed.

A MULTIPURPOSE HISTORIC CENTER

Where can you find swing dancing, bingo, and little league in the same distinctive structure?

Located at the corner of Amherst and Grant Streets, Polish Cadets, the "Meeting Place of Black Rock," was founded in 1899 and has been housed in its current building (designed by local Polish architect W. Zawadzki) since 1913. It is affiliated with nearby Assumption Church. Polish Cadets has a credit union on-site, hosts a lounge night on Friday (there are two bars), and is the site of a Dyngus Day celebration complete with folk dancing. It also acts as an advocacy group for the Black Rock neighborhood.

The Polish Cadets also hosts swing dancing clubs, focusing on the 6-count swing, Charleston, Balboa, and Lindy hop. Serious participants tend to dance in 1940s-style dress. It's a great example of how traditional private clubs have pivoted to embrace different cultural activities than those prevalent when they were founded.

POLISH CADETS

WHAT: Buffalo's Black Rock Polish cultural center

WHERE: 927 Grant St.

COST: There are various events, all reasonably priced. The lounge is open for drinks on Thursday and Fridays.

PRO TIP: The hall can be rented for all kinds of purposes.

Polish Cadets was founded in 1899 with the assistance of Reverend Adam Marcinkiewicz, the pastor of nearby Assumption Church.

Top: The Polish Cadets hosted many festivals and celebrations throughout the decades, many involving traditional costumes. Photo courtesy of the Buffalo History Museum.
Inset: Dancing at the club. Photo courtesy of Pixabay

HIKE THE RAVINES

Want some local history with your nature fix?

Once known as Larkin Woods, Franklin Gulf Park sits on the border between Eden and North Collins. Although the park is undeveloped, it's partially marked and noteworthy for its creeks and waterfalls. The red/orange path leads hikers past the foundations of a cottage once used by 19th-century industrialist John D. Larkin (1845–1926).

Larkin started out with one product, a bar of soap, and built that into a mail-order empire offering everything from furniture to clothing to tea. The company occupied 21 buildings in Buffalo's Seneca/Swan neighborhood.

There are plenty of better-known reminders of the Larkin days—notably Frank Lloyd Wright's buildings for a Larkin executive, Darwin Martin—but the obscure remains in Franklin Gulf Park speak to that completely unplugged time when retreating to the woods meant just that.

Enjoy Franklin Gulf's natural beauty with care; there are steep ravines and drop-offs, and it's important to bring a map and a compass, or a GPS-enabled device, just in case.

FRANKLIN GULF PARK

WHAT: A wild park connected with a mail-order pioneer

WHERE: Larkin Road, North Collins, NY

COST: Free

PRO TIP: Newbies should take a guided tour.

Western New Yorkers tend to flock to a few well-known beauty spots, but there are dozens of less-traveled parks and preserves that offer equal or even better experiences.

Ruins and geocaches add to the interest of this undeveloped park.
Photo by kc kratt photography

A REFUGE FOR RARE WATERFOWL

Think you know ducks?

This is the only waterfowl park in the US that is open to the public—there's even a gift shop! Founded in 1983 by conservationists Rosemary and Milton Miner on their own property, Gooseneck Hill is home to 300 geese, ducks, and swans, including many rare species. There are four wheelchair-accessible ponds, regular guided tours, and the two largest covered aviaries in the world.

GOOSENECK HILL WATERFOWL SANCTUARY

WHAT: A waterfowl sanctuary

WHERE: 5067 Townline Rd., Delevan, NY

COST: Free

PRO TIP: It's possible to adopt—and name—a bird for a donation.

The Miners started by taking in two male ducks that had wandered onto their property in Holland, New York (about a half hour south of Buffalo). They decided to get mates for the two birds and then branched out into geese. As their bird-raising hobby grew, they needed more property and moved further south to nearby Delevan in 1998, where the sanctuary is now. It very quickly became a priority to raise and protect rare and endangered waterfowl. Rosemary has traveled to Alaska four times, where she

Group visits to the sanctuary must be arranged by appointment, but yearly festive events are held every summer. Check the website, gooseneckhillwaterfowlfarm.com.

Over 300 ducks, geese, and swans live in the sanctuary. Photo courtesy of Gooseneck Hill

was able to collect the eggs of rare birds that have since become Gooseneck Hill residents.

Longtime Western New York naturalist Gerry Rising loves the preserve, noting: "Some of the Miner's species include Ross's, emperor, lesser white-fronted, red-breasted, bar-headed and cackling geese. The bar-headed, red-breasted, and lesser white-fronted geese are world listed as endangered."

A CULINARY LEGEND

Are these the most glorious stuffed peppers in the land?

The true secret of Billy Ogden's Stuffed Banana Peppers may be lost forever. The chef who invented them in 1990, Andy DiVincenzo, died in 2004, and the restaurant he cofounded and where he served the peppers, Bill Ogden's, has been closed for more than 10 years. Nonetheless, these peppers are strongly persistent in Buffalo's culinary culture, so much so that discussions of them are common on social media, and several local restaurants offer similar peppers that are said to emulate the Billy Ogden recipe.

Falley Allen, in Allentown, includes authentic "Billy Ogden" peppers on its eclectic menu. Tappo, on Ellicott, adds sausage to the four-cheese stuffing mixture, and tops the peppers with an egg. Osteria 166, downtown, sticks with a simpler ricotta and mozzarella mixture, upping the Southern Italian ante by adding marinara. Look for traditional stuffed peppers throughout the Buffalo red sauce scene; they may not be quite like Billy Ogden's but they're equally satisfying.

BILLY OGDEN'S STUFFED BANANA PEPPERS

WHAT: A beloved preparation from a short-lived restaurant

WHERE: Falley Allen, at 204 Allen St., and Santasiero's, at 1329 Niagara St.

COST: $5–10

PRO TIP: It's worth trying to make these yourself, with great peppers from your local sources.

In a city full of signature dishes, stuffed banana peppers may not seem like a big deal, but these are.

Stuffed banana peppers are a favorite local dish. Photo by kc kratt photography

Stuffed Banana Peppers

(recipe furnished to writer Christa Seychew by chef Chris Daigler, co-owner, Falley Allen. Originally published in *Buffalo Spree* magazine)

Pepper ingredients

6 banana peppers
1 tbsp. garlic, chopped
1 tbsp. parsley, chopped
¼ cup olive oil/canola blend
stuffing (recipe below)

Pepper stuffing

1 cup cream cheese
½ cup mozzarella, shredded
½ cup Parmesan, grated
½ cup Romano, grated
½ cup mascarpone
½ cup crumbly blue cheese, preferably gorgonzola
2 tsp. ground white pepper
1 tbsp. anchovy paste
¼ cup Italian bread crumbs
rustic Italian bread for serving

Directions

1. Prepare peppers at least one hour ahead of cooking time. To make stuffing, combine all six cheeses, white pepper, and anchovy paste using a paddle attachment in a kitchen mixer. Mix thoroughly. Gently fold in bread crumbs until the filling thickens. It's key that the stuffing be thick enough that it doesn't seep out of the pepper during cooking. Set aside.
2. Prepare peppers by snipping the stem ends off and removing the inside ribs and seeds to the best of your ability. Stuff the peppers gently so as to not break them in the process. Once the peppers are stuffed, refrigerate them for an hour or more. This allows the cheese to solidify, further reducing leakage during cooking. Remove the peppers from the fridge. Heat a large skillet on high heat. Add the oil blend. Be careful as the oil will spit and the peppers may, too.
3. Once the oil begins to smoke, add peppers immediately and sear both sides. The peppers will begin to ooze a little, but don't worry because the crispy bits at the end are the best part. Once seared, place the peppers on your serving plate, remove the pan from the heat, and add the garlic. Toast just a little; you don't want it to burn. Add parsley, toss, and then pour the oil, garlic, and parsley mixture over the peppers.

THE COURT WITH THE MOSTEST

Where can you see the true kings and queens of Buffalo?

Here's a group that knows how to put the fun into fundraising. Buffalo's Imperial Court can be seen front and center at many celebratory events, but don't let the wigs, Cuban heels, sequins, and satin fool you. The Court is a mainstay of Western New York LGBTQ life, and its ongoing mission is to support AIDS research and treatment throughout the world. If there's a cause or an event that needs support, chances are Imperial Court members will be there, in regalia or not.

Every year, a new emperor and empress are elected by the general membership and celebrated in a coronation gala, which, like all the Imperial Court's activities, is aimed at raising funds for deserving causes.

IMPERIAL COURT

WHAT: Buffalo's civic-minded queens and princes

WHERE: 266 Elmwood Ave. (mailing address)

COST: Events are fundraisers.

PRO TIP: Don't miss the May coronation event.

The Imperial Court of Buffalo was founded as part of the International Court System, a group of independent charities started in 1965 in San Francisco by José Sarria. Today, there are 65 chapters in the US, Canada, and Mexico, including Buffalo's.

Every May, a new emperor and empress are elected by the general membership as part of a charitable gala. Photo courtesy of the Imperial Court of Buffalo

José Sarria, who founded the first Imperial Court in San Francisco in 1965, preceded Harvey Milk as the first openly gay individual to run for public office in the United States. One of the past Emperors of New York City, Fredd E. "Tree" Sequoia, was bartending at the Stonewall Inn on the night of the historic 1969 riots, and still bartends there to this day.

A CREEK RUNS THROUGH IT

Want to try for a steelhead?

About an hour south of Buffalo, two preserves on Canadaway Creek, near Fredonia, offer waterfalls, creeks, ponds, woodlands, and well-marked trails, as well as the best steelhead trout fishing anglers will find anywhere: better, even, than on the nationally famous Salmon River. Birdwatchers should keep their binoculars trained on the yellow-bellied sapsuckers and great blue herons, as well as many other species, that nest here.

Artist, naturalist, and writer Alberto Rey has described his first encounter with Canadaway: "I found myself standing near the mouth of the Canadaway with a fly rod in hand not knowing what I was doing and with little idea of how much there was to learn. I soon saw some splashing downstream, and, to my amazement, I saw my first bright-red sockeye salmon in the distance furiously struggling in the low water to make its way around the rocks as it moved upstream."

CANADAWAY CREEK WILDLIFE MANAGEMENT AREA

WHAT: Great fishing and scenery south of the city

WHERE: Arkwright, NY

COST: Free

PRO TIP: Be sure to work with one of many fishing guides operating in Western New York.

Alberto Rey: "One of the wonderful qualities about fly-fishing is that it can put you in the middle of a beautiful natural environment for hours at a time. You can notice how the world around you changes."

Canadaway Creek offers fishing and hiking. Photo courtesy of Alberto Rey

The 2,000 acres of the Canadaway Creek WMA also provide a rare opportunity for nonfishermen to hike in a dense conifer and hardwood forest studded with ravines. This wild area is picturesque in all seasons and only minutes away from the nearest thruway exit.

ANOTHER GREAT ESCAPE

Where can you get both political history and wild scenery?

Those who have ever thrilled to the long, precarious wooden footbridges often seen in adventure films will love visiting Royalton Ravine, where an 80-foot-long wooden suspension bridge crosses Eighteen Mile Creek. Unlike the movies, the bridge is only a few feet over the creek, so there's not much danger.

Other highlights of this pretty picnic spot include a 25-foot waterfall alongside the ruins of a homestead that once belonged to Belva Lockwood, an attorney, women's rights activist, and the first woman to run for president of the United States (in 1884 and 1888).

Lockwood was born in Royalton in 1830. Along with her presidential run, she was the first woman to practice law before the Supreme Court Bar and the first woman to be nominated to the US Court of Claims. The walls of her former home, although deteriorating, still stand and are an interesting historic element within this lovely natural setting. In addition to a 43-year career as an attorney, Lockwood was a well-respected writer, who frequently wrote essays about women's suffrage

ROYALTON RAVINE

WHAT: A beautiful park notable for its swinging footbridge

WHERE: Gasport Road, Gasport, NY

COST: Free

PRO TIP: This park is only open in summer.

Though most visitors to Royalton Ravine are likely unaware of Belva Lockwood, her story adds a rich note of history to a lovely natural spot.

Walk through history in Royalton. Photo by Holly Metz Doyle

and the need for legal equality for many publications, including *Cosmopolitan* (then a journal of current issues), the *American Magazine of Civics*, *Harper's Weekly*, and *Lippincott's*.

THE GORGE IS THE THING

Think you've really seen Niagara Falls?

Taking out-of-town visitors to Niagara Falls can get kind of old. Too often, the excursion consists of a quick drive to Prospect Point on the US side or a race over the border to get a close-up view of the Horseshoe Falls at Niagara Falls, Ontario. Neither of these vantage points offer much more than crowds and mist, when all's said and done.

Niagara Falls and the Niagara River Gorge offer much more than the average visitor ever glimpses, especially the Whirlpool Rapids and Devil's Hole. The ferocious waves of the Niagara River continue beyond the Falls all the way to Devil's Hole, which can be part of a hike starting at the Whirlpool Rapids. The hike is moderately difficult, with the difficult part consisting mainly of the walk down to the river from Whirlpool State Park and the walk up at Devil's Hole State Park. Otherwise, there is a decent path along the river that is studded with old-growth trees, spectacular rock formations, and wildflowers. In good weather, it's possible to venture out to large formations and take a break, perhaps enjoying a picnic lunch.

GORGE WALK

WHAT: The best way to understand Niagara Falls

WHERE: Start from either Whirlpool State Park or Devil's Hole State Park, Niagara Falls, NY.

COST: Free

PRO TIP: Take this trip in good weather; slippery trails and rocks have led to accidents.

The Niagara River doesn't calm down after the Falls—far from it. Many find the crashing waves, swirling eddies, and majestic rocks of the lower Niagara equally as exciting.

The hike to the bottom of the gorge is rewarded by a close-up look at churning whirlpools and leaping waves. Photo by kc kratt photography

A local who frequently hikes the gorge says, "The amazing thing here is that I can walk out my door and in 20 minutes I can be at the bottom of the gorge, looking at a 1,500-year-old spruce, watching salmon jump in the river, completely surrounded by this great icon of nature, but if I go in another direction, in 10 minutes I can be in an urban environment, on a walkable Main Street, near a bookstore, dry cleaner, and florist. How many places are there where you can do that?"

Devil's Hole was supposedly given its name when the Senecas told early European explorers that it was the abode of the evil spirit and that its difficult terrain had been created as a punishment.

THE MIGHTY ZOAR

Where else can you find magnificent canyons, 14 waterfalls, and red-spotted newts?

From white water rafting to peaceful tubing to strenuous hiking, Zoar Valley has it all. The major natural features include an old-growth forest and a deep, 415-feet canyon, with Cattaraugus Creek running through them.

Explorers can choose to follow paths at the bottom of the canyon, near the water, or try for higher elevations. From high or low, the views are equally spectacular. There are many, many options, including some short hikes through the creek in summer that can be combined with picnics. The most popular and easiest access is from the Valentine Flats parking area and the Forty Road parking area. Keep an eye out for wildlife, including broad-winged hawks, American kestrels, red-bellied woodpeckers, woodchucks, foxes, Midland painted turtles, and red-spotted newts.

Hikers climbing the sides of the canyon need to exercise caution; be sure to research well, and print out maps and

ZOAR VALLEY

WHAT: An impressive canyon filled with natural beauty

WHERE: Zoar Valley Multiple Use Area, towns of Otto, Persia, and Collins, NY

COST: Free

PRO TIP: The New York State Department of Environmental Conservation has strict rules and regulations governing this site. Check them out to avoid disappointment at dec.ny.gov/lands/36931.html.

This is undoubtedly one of the wildest areas in Western New York, but it's less than an hour from downtown Buffalo.

Wet feet are the worst that will happen hiking along the bottom of the gorge. Photo by Stephen Gabris

instructions before visiting, and keep on marked trails. Zoar's danger is one of the reasons it remains obscure and uncrowded, but that danger should be respected. Oh—and ignore any websites that mention "nude beaches" or advise jumping off waterfalls. This information is out of date, and the activities mentioned are illegal.

THIS IS ONLY A TEST

When is a flower more than just a pretty face?

It's no secret that the Erie Basin Marina is a colorful beacon of floral activity from May through September. Anyone visiting this popular spot to board a vessel, grab a hot dog, or just hang out in the sun will immediately notice the vibrant beds of petunias, dahlias, geraniums, and other annuals, as well as large container plantings, lining the walkways. Most observers assume this is a municipal beautification effort, but the flowers actually are there for testing purposes.

Seeds are sent to head gardener Stan Swisher, who germinates them in a greenhouse and then plants the seedlings out in the waterfront beds. These are varieties not yet released for the commercial market, and they have been sent here to see if they will withstand the full sun and lake winds of this location. There are very few such trial gardens in the US; Buffalonians should be proud that one of them is on their waterfront. Sadly, very few are aware.

ERIE BASIN MARINA TRIAL GARDENS

WHAT: A beautiful public garden with a purpose

WHERE: 329 Erie St.

COST: Free

PRO TIP: Look for Stan, who's on the job most weekdays.

One man, Stan Swisher, has been keeping the Erie Basin Marina Trial Gardens going for more than 40 years. His secret? He's crazy.

It's impossible to take common annuals, even marigolds, for granted after a visit to the Test Gardens. Photo by Elizabeth Licata

There remains a certain snobbishness about annuals, partly because some perceive them as "common," and partly because they're, well, annual. But we defy anyone to scorn annuals after seeing the magnificent work here. They are huge, floriferous, healthy, and interesting: black and gold double petunias, a Crystal Sky variety that's subtler than many of the speckled petunias, and a new petunia/calibrachoa hybrid. There is a big difference between these and nursery-bought annuals. Western New York has summers made for annuals: hot with plenty of rain.

LOOK UP

Which domed ceiling is also a magnificent work of art that most have never seen?

Buffalo Savings Bank, now a branch of M&T Bank, is known mainly for its shimmering gold dome and the other Beaux Arts architectural elements that mark it as an 1899 masterpiece by the Buffalo firm of Green and Wicks. The dome is rightly famous; its last restoration in 1998 involved 140,000 paper-thin sheets of 23.75-carat gold leaf. The rest of the exterior architecture lives up to the dome's magnificence, including its Corinthian columns, pilasters, capitals, and massive fanlights.

Each column took three months to complete, and the structure contained more large granite stones than any building in the US at the time. The interior also is replete with ornamentation—with its own columns, pilasters, pediments, and balconies—and while visitors might be forgiven for failing to look all the way up at the interior side of the gold dome and its four supporting pendentives—they should. Each triangular pendentive is a symbolic representation of a Buffalo strength: Industry, The Arts, Commerce, and Power. Power is probably the most direct of the four as it depicts Niagara Falls. Above these, the large central dome includes neoclassic depictions of the signs of the Zodiac.

Murals also cover the upper walls of the north and east wings; these include idealized versions of Native American figures, such as Seneca chiefs Red Jacket and Farmer's Brother (Honayewus), engaged in treaties with Buffalo's European settlers. All told, there are enough narrative murals, vignettes, and general painted

---

Part of the rotunda mural declares, "Virtue is the Root and Wealth the Flower." It's a sentiment you might expect to find decorating the inside of a bank.

The central dome features signs of the Zodiac. Photo by Jean-Pierre Thimot

GOLD DOME MURALS

WHAT: Symbolic murals on the ceiling of a gorgeous bank building

WHERE: M&T Bank's Fountain Plaza Branch, 545 Main St.

COST: Free

PRO TIP: Consider a tour, offered year-round by explorebuffalo.org.

decoration to reward hours of study. It would all take up at least two big rooms of a museum. The artistic firm that completed all this included artists William C. Francis (of Buffalo), Eugene F. Savage, and George Davidson, who already had completed many significant commissions. These decorations were somewhat of an afterthought; they were completed in 1926, more than 25 years after the completion of the building.

THE WILDEST CITY HALL IN THE US

Can you say Native-American-inspired masterpiece?

Its institutional function, lack of parking, and the general gloom inside might deter many from thoroughly exploring the interior of this astounding structure, but everyone should get past all that and celebrate one of Buffalo's most fascinating feats of design. Here are just five reasons to celebrate Buffalo City Hall as one of the most important—and symbolic—pieces of architecture in the US:

1. Hugh Ferriss, American architect, illustrator, poet, and author of *The Metropolis of Tomorrow* (1922), was a huge influence on architects of this time. His dramatic illustrations of buildings with setback, thinner towers (required by New York City law then), lit up at night, were the model for many Art Deco structures, including City Hall, as well as for Batman's Gotham City.
2. City Hall's mountain-like shape is inspired by nature, and the top of the structure is meant to resemble an Indian headdress. This upper portion is covered with brightly colored, terra-cotta ornamental elements.
3. The Common Council Chambers is lit by a large, golden, sunburst window, while around the sides, large columns are topped with figures representing 12 virtues. These originally were supposed to be busts of prominent Buffalonians, but nobody could agree on who was worthy.
4. It would take hours to thoroughly unpack the history and symbolism embedded in the lobby murals and lunettes painted by William de Leftwich Dodge, which refer to Buffalo's founding, location, and the region's most important industries, as well as representations of education, civil service, construction, and more.
5. The observation deck offers a 360-degree view of Buffalo, with Niagara Falls and Toronto, Ontario, in the distance.

Buffalo City Hall.
Photo by Steve Rosenthal

CITY HALL

WHAT: A municipal structure that's equally important as a work of art

WHERE: Niagara Square

COST: Free tours are offered on weekdays at noon.

PRO TIP: Council meetings are usually open to the public.

The building was started September 16, 1929, completed November 10, 1931, and dedicated July 1, 1932, to commemorate Buffalo's centennial.

The 32-story-high structure was built on two triangular lots on the west side of Niagara Square, spanning Court Street. Its construction closed off Court Street from the square, the first interruption of Joseph Ellicott's street plan. The completion of the similarly styled Art Deco State and Federal Buildings in 1935 on the east side of Niagara Square realized the concept of a city center group of governmental buildings, first suggested in 1920.

City Hall's decorative art illustrates significant elements in the area's history. Some of the facade depictions include these:

- Themes of the Iroquois Indian nation
- The development of the Erie Canal
- The US's relationship with Canada
- The pioneering and industrial spirit of Buffalo's citizens, past and present

Included are statues of Buffalonians who became US presidents: Millard Fillmore and Grover Cleveland.

In spite of the destructive relationship that already had been clearly established between indigenous peoples and their European conquerors, the design of Dietel & Wade's City Hall was based firmly on visual themes connected to the Iroquois Nation.

BUFFALO IS FULL OF IT

How did a bologna sandwich finally gain respect?

In Buffalo, it's called fried bologna, not a bologna sandwich, and it regains the respect that this highly seasoned Italian pork sausage has lost in its journey from authentic artisanal product to commercial luncheon meat. The slices can be cut thin or thick and can be grilled as well as fried. It depends on the venue. The main thing is that bologna is treated with the care that it deserves. Food writer Arthur Bovino (author of *Buffalo Everything: A Guide to Eating in "The Nickel City"*) says, "You'll find it on the menu of most sandwich shops and pizzerias."

Though bologna technically originates in Italy (as mortadella), it was popular with German and Polish immigrants to Buffalo. Though traditional mortadella could not be imported or copied, German immigrants started making bologna using pork as well as other meats of all types. This product was cheap and easily portable for laborer's lunches. There has

FRIED (OR GRILLED) BOLOGNA SANDWICH

WHAT: A longtime local favorite

WHERE: Throughout Buffalo, with a standout example at Sophia's Restaurant, 749 Military Rd.

COST: About $10 or less

PRO TIP: Cutting slits into the bologna before cooking helps it brown evenly.

Certain restaurants in Buffalo have transformed a lunchbox sandwich meant to be endured more than savored into a respected treat. It's on the menu in many sandwich shops, Polish eateries, and pizzerias, as well as a high-end, farm-to-table restaurant.

Top: Lunch meat turns into a delicacy at Sophia's. Photo by Elizabeth Licata. Inset: Fried bologna sandwich. Photo by kc kratt photography

been a bologna backlash in many parts of America, but, in Buffalo, bologna never left.

As Bovino says: "I fell in love with the late-night fried bologna sandwich served at Toutant while doing research on my book. At Toutant, they bake their own bread, spend two days making the bologna from scratch, and marinate the onions in Genesee beer. Two three-quarter inch thick slices get covered in onions and ooey-gooey white American cheese. At least three slices.

You'd have to tear me away from digging into one of these—along with a frozen tasty drink."

GUARDED BY A MOUNTAIN LION

Why do some critics call the architecture of this structure "aggressive"?

Known as the Bemis-Ransom House, this building was designed by Edward Silsbee, Frank Lloyd Wright's first employer. The Bemis-Ransom House lives on North Street, along with many of Buffalo's most notable mansions. Built in 1883, the structure is technically Queen Anne, but it has steeply soaring rooflines, arcaded porches, and strong Romanesque elements that add to its dramatic presence on the streetscape—not to mention the two catamounts (mountain lions) that sit attentively on the central and west elevations.

The house was built for Buffalo lumber baron John Bemis and his family. Although it's now offices, the building's interior

BEMIS-RANSOM HOUSE

WHAT: A distinctive mansion that stands out on a street of mansions

WHERE: 267 North St.

COST: Tours are offered occasionally by explorebuffalo.org; check the website for pricing.

PRO TIP: This block contains some of Buffalo's more historic structures.

Many of the distinctive structures that started as private homes now host nonprofit organizations and law firms. Though the interiors have been altered, many important historic elements survive from their former lives as residences.

Look closely at this mansion for dramatic elements. Photos by Nancy J. Parisi

retains many original elements, including colorful encaustic floor tiles, oak wainscoting, stained glass windows, magnificent fireplaces, an elaborate staircase, and, upstairs, the Middle Eastern room, which is enclosed in an exotic pavilion covered in Islamic calligraphy decorations.

A HIGH SCHOOL GYMNASIUM LOADED WITH HISTORY

What Masonic consistory hosted a Gregg Allman concert?

In 1925, the Freemasons bought the former Rand family mansion, part of Delaware Avenue's "mansion row," with the intention of transforming it into its new consistory. They added a new foyer, a bowling alley, Turkish baths, and a 6,000-square-foot auditorium. This was ornamented with 10 Corinthian columns along the walls, ceiling molding and murals surrounded by Tiffany stained glass, and a huge balcony, the largest freestanding balcony of its time in the US. The Masonic double-headed eagle appears above the stage.

When the Masons could no longer pay taxes on this structure, it was taken over by the city and used for performances, eventually serving as a temporary home for the Buffalo Philharmonic, as the orchestra waited for Kleinhans Music Hall to be finished. The building was purchased by Canisius High School in 1944, the orchestra pit was covered up, and it was converted to the Scaccia Auditorium, which hosted many games, concerts, assemblies, and other school events.

CANISIUS AUDITORIUM

WHAT: A former mansion transformed by the Masons

WHERE: 1180 Delaware Ave.

COST: Free, with permission from the school

PRO TIP: The Canisius College campus, nearby on Main Street, is also worth exploring.

The late Gregg Allman, of the Allman Brothers Band, in Buffalo for drug treatment, performed a surprise, hour-long afternoon concert here in 1976. A few Canisius students had discovered that Allman was in town and wrote letters to the singer at his Buffalo address. Allman was touched by the letters and also was longing to perform. His wife, Cher, sat on the stage with

The high school auditorium where a recovering Gregg Allman performed. Photo by Stephen Gabris

children Chastity (now Chaz) and Elijah Blue. In later life, Allman was to recall the concert with great fondness. Canisius built a new athletic facility in 2009, but the beautiful auditorium is still used for special events.

The term “consistory” is also used in the Roman Catholic administrative hierarchy, but the Masons use it in reference to the Sublime Princes of the Royal Secret, originally an order of knighthood.

A SECLUDED SHORELINE SPOT

Why is Buffalo's closest beach located in Canada?

Buffalo's inland sea, Lake Erie, is lined with industrial ruins, shale cliffs, private residences, and—here and there—public beaches. Thanks to the ease of driving across the Peace Bridge to Lake Erie's Canadian shore, a few of the Canadian beaches are actually closer than those on the American side, which start well south of the city.

The nearest Canadian beach is the charming getaway of Waverley Beach, which is surrounded by wooded nature trails and is considered the eastern terminus of the Friendship Trail. There's also a great view of the Buffalo skyline and windmills. This was the site of the Erie Beach Amusement Park, and remnants remain of the popular turn-of-the-century attraction, which closed in 1930. There are few amenities: just free parking, bike trails, and restrooms. In 1885, Buffalonians seeking relaxation and entertainment would sail over to have a picnic in this obscure spot that was then known as Snake Hill Grove.

WAVERLEY BEACH

WHAT: Buffalo's secret beach across the border

WHERE: 271 St. Helena St., Fort Erie, Ontario, Canada

COST: Free (passport or enhanced ID required at the border)

PRO TIP: Wear shoes at all times.

The Canadian coastline of Lake Erie, mere minutes away from downtown, is lined with summer homes owned by Buffalonians. These "cottages" are generally two-story, multi-bedroom homes with all the amenities.

Take in the beauty of Lake Erie and get a great view of the Buffalo skyline.
Photo by kc kratt photography

By 1930, the park's last year of operation, thousands of visitors a day would arrive by steamship to ride a roller coaster as big as any in North America. The park's filtered lake-water pool was proclaimed as the world's largest outdoor pool. This beauty spot's demise came is a result of the Great Depression. It was simply abandoned to the elements and was reclaimed by nature over the next few decades.

GET ON THE BUS

Who does the best tours of old-timey Buffalo?

Forgotten Buffalo Bus Tours are immersive experiences that include stops at bars and restaurants, live music performances, and other elements that go far beyond the usual narrated tour. The tours focus on Buffalo's historic ethnic culture, particularly Polish American Buffalo and the neighborhood known as Broadway-Fillmore or Polonia. The bar stops focus on family-owned taverns known for their holiday gatherings, traditional music (think polka), and hearty Polish offerings such as kielbasa and pierogi. The tours don't neglect historic architecture either, especially as many of Buffalo's most beautiful churches are in this neighborhood.

A typical tour takes four to five hours and includes a meal and entertainment as well as lively narration from tour guides Marty Biniasz and Eddy Dobosiewicz. Biniasz is well versed in Buffalo history and has written books on various local topics. In addition to the Polonia tours, there are tours focusing on Irish Buffalo, ethnic clubs, and classic taverns.

FORGOTTEN BUFFALO TOURS

WHAT: A tour company focusing on nostalgia and ethnic pride

WHERE: forgottenbuffalo.com

COST: $50 a person, on average

PRO TIP: This is a great idea for a group of friends or work colleagues.

One of the most popular trips recreates an authentic Polish Christmas Eve circa 1964, complete with a traditional Wigilia supper, a visit to a historic church, and Christmas caroling.

St. Stanislaus Church, the Mother Church of Polonia. Photo by kc kratt photography

One of Forgotten Buffalo's most popular slogans is "It's not bar hopping if it's done for educational purposes!" On its website, the tour organization declares, "Forgotten Buffalo hopes to provide visitors with a uniquely Buffalo experience. Visit sites that have been left behind, or perhaps clandestinely left in place, providing clues as to what was there before. In an age where life continually looks at renewing and reinventing itself every few decades, Forgotten Buffalo takes pride in the Niagara Frontier's triumphal past. . . . More than just a nostalgic trip through time, Forgotten Buffalo allows you to better understand why Buffalo is one of the most unique urban communities in the world."

THE BAR WITH NO STOOLS

What makes this 130-year-old watering hole a fan favorite?

Just to be clear, there was never a conscious decision to eschew stools at this popular Southtowns joint. It didn't have them when it opened in 1881 (as archival photos show) and doesn't have them now.

WALLENWEIN'S HOTEL

WHAT: A distinctive traditional tavern

WHERE: 641 Oakwood Ave., East Aurora, NY

COST: Price of a drink

PRO TIP: Belly up to the bar, and start a conversation.

Wallenwein's started out as a modest hotel, but, thanks to an early focus on beer brewing and bottling, the tavern side took over. Pictures of the tavern in the 1880s and images now show a surprisingly similar exterior: even the bar is easily recognizable 100 years later. In addition to its lack of stools, the tavern is known for other quirks, including the fact that it was the first place to serve pizza in East Aurora and that its limburger cheese sandwiches are strangely popular. A large cohort of faithful regulars comes in every Thursday for spaghetti night, which features the chef's homemade sauce and the owner's homemade meatballs. Many charity events are hosted or supported here. In a recent *Buffalo News* interview, owner Ben Holmes explained, "It's not a hip bar, but it's hip not to be a hip bar."

Many feel the lack of stools makes the bar friendlier; the crowd at the bar parts easily to let newcomers belly up and order their drinks. There's also a lot more room for socializing.

Top: It's always standing room only at Wallenwein's. Photo by kc kratt photography. Inset: Wallenwein's in th early days. Photo courtesy of Wallenwein's Hotel

GLORY TO THE HEROES

Why does Buffalo treasure its two Ukrainian centers?

The modest Ukrainian-American Civic Center (in northwest Buffalo, near the Niagara River) and the majestic Dnipro Ukrainian Cultural Center (on the East Side) are bulwarks of Ukrainian culture. The first is open to the public on Thursdays and Fridays, while the second welcomes nonmembers during special public events. While the Civic Center has transitioned into more of a purely social club, Dnipro hosts a library, credit union, language school, and dance troupe.

Dnipro is known for its elegant ballroom, featuring 26-foot ceilings, murals, and a majestic stage. For decades, almost anything important that happened in the Ukrainian American community in Buffalo happened at Dnipro, or was intensely discussed at Dnipro. It's named after the largest river in the Ukraine.

In addition to its traditional service to Buffalo's Ukrainian American community, Dnipro has become popular as a location for offbeat parties and fundraisers for such organizations as the Squeaky Wheel Film & Media Arts Center and Torn Space Theater, which, until recently, made Dnipro the home of its popular "Prom of the Dead" Halloween event.

DNIPRO UKRAINIAN CULTURAL CENTER & UKRAINIAN-AMERICAN CIVIC CENTER

WHAT: Two places where Buffalo's Ukrainian heritage is celebrated and kept alive

WHERE: 562 Genesee St.; 205 Military Rd.

COST: Price of a drink, but not always open to nonmembers

PRO TIP: Check ForgottenBuffalo.com for guided tours.

Dnipro Center. Photo courtesy of Dnipro

Two important waves of immigration from the Ukraine to Western New York occurred, one beginning around 1900 and the next during World War II, as many Ukrainians were displaced from their homeland. Many Ukrainians in Buffalo maintain ties to their war-torn homeland, hoping for full independence and peace.

WHERE TO WATCH A SUNSET

How best to spend a beautiful summer evening?

The Lake Erie coastline is beautiful year-round, but waterfront restaurants sometimes have trouble convincing customers to appreciate that fact. Public House on the Lake, one of three Public House venues in the area, is located in a spot that long has hosted waterfront dining venues. It is easily one of the top five places to see a sunset in the area.

PUBLIC HOUSE ON THE LAKE

WHAT: A lakeside restaurant with spectacular views

WHERE: 914 Lakeshore Blvd., Hamburg, NY

COST: Price of a drink

PRO TIP: Go on a weekday to grab a seat by the water.

Those who hold stereotypical views of Buffalo would find it difficult to recognize the beachy, island vibe of Public House, which hosts mellow musical entertainment on its expansive deck, as the waves crash on the shore below. There's also an outdoor bar on the spacious property, with plenty of space for dining inside and out. Most have no idea this Buffalo exists.

Before Frank and Sara Testa took over this space in 2015, it had been occupied by Root 5 since 1992. Before that, it was Inn on the Lake from 1972 to 1992. As is a trend in current restaurant culture, the Testas had already tested their concepts on Buffalo's Public House and have added another Public House in Ellicottville.

Waterfront restaurants here have to deal with an inhospitable winter climate, which makes long-term survival a bit tricky, but sunset views don't depend on temperatures.

Waterfront sunsets are a lovely way to end the day. Photos by Eric Frick

The website OnlyinYourState.com recommends Chestnut Ridge State Park, the Outer Harbor, the Ferris Wheel at the Erie County State Fair, the patio at Pearl Street Pub, Delaware Park, and Golden Hill State Park as other spots offering glorious sunset views. Many Buffalo commuters get a daily spectacle as they drive along 190 South on their way home, once daylight savings time ends in the fall.

NOT JUST ANOTHER DIVE

Why is this seedy watering hole so beloved?

Every town probably has dozens of nondescript, shot-and-a-beer taverns, with (mainly) neighborhood-based regulars filling the barstools daily. We're not talking about that kind of dive. Nor do we refer to the type of dive that has manufactured its funky ambiance, adds touches of tongue-in-cheek decor regularly, and maintains a merchandise display.

There are no souvenir T-shirts at the Old Pink, 223 Allen St. This 36-year-old bar has been a destination for students, artists, writers, musicians, and anyone looking for something different ever since it opened its doors. Though he no longer owns the bar, the Pink's enduring dot-alt character is the creation of its founder, Mark Supples, who's responsible for starting a tradition of great DJs and attracting a diverse crowd, including visiting rock stars. The bar is covered with a flame-dominated mural on the outside, while every surface of the interior is covered in graffiti, posters, stickers, and an accumulation of miscellaneous decor that's been growing over the years—not bulk-purchased from a warehouse.

In a city with a hard-partying reputation, the Old Pink still stands out. It's even attracted national notice, making several lists of distinctive dives and listed as worthy of preservation by the National Trust for Historic Preservation.

OLD PINK/223 ALLEN

WHAT: Buffalo's best dive bar

WHERE: 223 Allen St.

COST: Price of a drink

PRO TIP: There is no printed menu, but ask about the steak sandwich.

Top: While the dark interior, with its lurid red lights, hasn't changed much over the years, some of the amenities, such as the restrooms, have not stood up well to being preserved in their vintage states. Surviving a trip to the ladies room here is considered a badge of honor. Photo by Joe George. Inset: Flames are painted on the bar's entrance. Photo by kc kratt photography

---

"The bar's blue and purple paint job, dotted with snowy clouds and bright green flames, is hard to miss in downtown Buffalo, New York."—from the National Trust for Historic Preservation's #savethedivebar campaign

A THREE-STORY PARADISE FOR READERS

Who says print is dead?

This treasure trove has a great travel section, an entire section devoted to all things Niagara Falls, and a cool selection of novelty gifts by the cash register.

The largest independent bookstore in Western New York is located on a rundown section of Niagara Fall's Main Street; that's why many locals have still never been there. It's their loss. The spacious aisles of the Book Corner offer hours of browsing, with new books and local interest on the main floor, used fiction above, and used nonfiction below.

Owner Jeffrey Scott Morrow says that his customers—who often come from all over the globe, thanks to the Niagara Falls location—are usually amazed by the size and character of the store, which has a large community space with a baby grand piano on the second floor. Anyone accustomed to the cookie-cutter

THE BOOK CORNER

WHAT: A temple of books, old and new

WHERE: 1801 Main St., Niagara Falls

COST: Free, outside of purchases

PRO TIP: Combine a trip here with a visit to the nearby Underground Railroad Heritage Center.

The original bookshop was founded in 1927 and came to its current location in 1982. Current owner Jeff Morrow bought it from his father in 2001.

The shops windows are papered with fascinating posters and printed matter. Photos by Elizabeth Licata

look and feel of bookstore chains isn't ready for the Book Corner: its idiosyncratic owner is almost always on the premises, ready to offer friendly remarks and recommendations, and it's possible to get lost upstairs, where myriad rooms featuring romance, mystery, sci-fi, and general fiction open in and out of each other. It's hard to imagine a more delightful experience than paging through a used novel by a second-floor window in the Book Corner, with the sunshine streaming in and a resident cat walking by.

LIFE UNDERGROUND

Want to take a spooky stroll through 19th-century industry?

In 1858, a tunnel was blasted out of solid rock by Birdsill Holly, the mechanical genius who channeled the Erie Canal to provide water power for Lockport, 20 miles north of Buffalo. Much of this water was used for fire protection, as part of a system Holly created. His Holly System of Water Supply and Fire Protection was being used in more than 100 US cities by 1881 and eventually was brought to 2,000 cities in the US and Canada. This also was the first tunnel to be used for hydraulic power.

In addition to powering Holly's operations, the Hydraulic Race Company also powered various local manufacturing companies. The last factory relying on this power closed in 1941, and the tunnel was inaccessible until it was rediscovered in the 1970s. Visitors now can tour it from May through October. The guided tour is mainly on foot, with a short boat ride, takes about 70

LOCKPORT CAVE AND UNDERGROUND BOAT RIDE

WHAT: A spooky and historic tour

WHERE: 5 Gooding St., Lockport, NY

COST: $17.50 (adults)

PRO TIP: This is not handicapped-accessible, and sturdy walking shoes are recommended.

This tour explores a man-made cave, but Lockport is known for a mysterious natural cave that exists mainly as a legend. Nobody has been able to explore it or pinpoint its exact location.

Top: The tunnels were used for water power and fire protection. Photo courtesy of sk via Flickr. Inset: Cave entrance. Photo courtesy of bobistraveling via Flickr

minutes, and includes the Erie Canal Flight of Five Locks and locks 34 and 35. Expect close-up views of underground rock formations, stalactites, and historic artifacts, with everything explained by the knowledgeable guides. There are also haunted tours at Halloween and lantern-lit evening tours. For those looking for aboveground excitement, the tour company offers a zip line trip across the Erie Canal and back.

A MAGICAL BACKROOM

Could this be Buffalo's most wildly decorated public space?

It hardly seems possible that the murals covering the ceiling and walls of Tabernacle were created by someone who had never painted before, but that's the truth. Sweet_ness 7 owner Prish Moran had planned to give the space for her new, café-adjacent bar/restaurant a simple paint job before proceeding with murals, so she asked an employee to take a roller to the space. After being shown how to use the roller and scaffolding, line cook Jeremy Twiss covered the walls with intricate figures and designs, working over several months to create an awe-inspiring restaurant interior. The Tabernacle serves dinner and drinks and hosts regular live music—jazz, folk, blues, Americana, and more.

Secret spots and backroom hideaways have always been the stuff of late night legend in Buffalo. Probably the most famous such spot, though long-closed, is

THE TABERNACLE AT SWEET_NESS 7 CAFÉ

WHAT: An illustrated backroom bar

WHERE: 211 Grant St.

COST: Price of a drink

PRO TIP: The café in this complex is a great daytime hangout, with delicious breakfast options and an equally cool vibe.

The complex was vacant and boarded up when owner Prish Moran took it on in 2007. It now includes four storefronts, seven large apartments, and a rooftop garden as well as the Tabernacle.

Murals beautify the outside. Photo by Stephen Gabris

the Rendezvous Bar & Grill on Niagara Street, also known as Johnny's Rendezvous. In its earliest iteration, this tavern only admitted patrons known to the proprietor, and one of the signs on the wall said "Only two drinks to a customer. No gentleman or lady will ask for three."

MOURN A LOST MASTERPIECE

Is this Buffalo's greatest shame? Worse than McKinley?

The demolition of the Larkin Soap Company Administration Building is considered by many as the single greatest avoidable loss of an architectural gem in the history of the United States.

Frank Lloyd Wright designed every detail of this 1906 five-story building himself; it was loaded with innovations such as full air-conditioning, a rooftop courtyard, built-in furniture, sound-absorption technology, and much more. A glass-roofed light court filled the central area, providing light to all the floors. About 1,800 clerks, secretaries, and executives worked here at the height of the Larkin mail-order company's success.

In the late twenties, business began to decline, and the company shut down in 1943. The building passed to the city of Buffalo, which did try to market it, even paying for a national

LARKIN ADMINISTRATION BUILDING REMNANT

WHAT: A brick pier from one of the most famous demolitions in the US

WHERE: Across the street from 700 Seneca, near parking lot

COST: Free

PRO TIP: It's just a brick pier. Combine this with other Larkinville activities.

It cost $4 million to create the building in 1906. In 1949, it was sold for $8,000 for a parking lot, and demolished a few months later.

Top: The old Larkin Soap Company. Photo courtesy of the Buffalo History Museum. Inset: A single brick pier remains from the foundation of the Larkin building. Photo by kc kratt photography

advertising campaign. By the end of the decade, the city had become discouraged and no longer had the will to fight for the building's survival. It had fallen into disrepair and was demolished (with difficulty). A single brick pier from the foundation remains and can be viewed.

BUFFALO AND THE MOB

Can Buffalo compete with Chicago and New York City as a major location for organized crime?

Entire books already have been written about organized crime in Western New York, which was so extensive—reaching into Canada, Pennsylvania, and other New York State locations—that it's difficult to summarize. A few basic details illustrate the extent of the activity.

BUFFALO AND THE MOB

WHAT: Organized crime in Buffalo, in a tour package

WHERE: Take one or all three of explorebuffalo.com's mob tours (Downtown, Allentown, and West Side).

COST: $15

PRO TIP: Though many of the original locations for mob activity (Laborers 210, the Apalachin residence) can be located, it's much better to go on a lively, narrated tour that fills in the details of what took place. Otherwise, these are just buildings.

The "Apalachin Meeting," on November 14, 1957, was planned by Stefano Magaddino, a Niagara Falls–based crime boss. It included about 100 members of the Mafia Commission and was held at the country home of Joseph Barbara, a Magaddino soldier, who lived about 200 miles southeast of Buffalo. Attendees included such figures as Joe Bonnano, Vito Genovese, and "Lucky" Luciano. However, state police were alerted to the gathering and raided it, making many arrests. None of these led to convictions at the time, but the raid exposed Mafia activities to the public in a way they never had been before. Famously, this event forced J. Edgar Hoover to admit that there might be organized crime in America.

Magaddino, known as "The Undertaker," started out supplying liquor to speakeasies in Buffalo and Niagara Falls during Prohibition, and then moved on to loan-sharking, illegal gambling, extortion, and labor racketeering, as

Mob activity in the 1960s. Photo courtesy of the Courier Express archives

well as legitimate businesses. He maintained control over his extensive territory for more than 50 years and was the longest-tenured boss in the history of the American Mafia. He finally was arrested in 1968, and his reign ended in 1969; he didn't serve any lengthy jail time, but the police found almost $500,000 in his family's possession, which led to dissension among his allies. He died in 1974.

After Magaddino's reign, activity continued, with a local union, Laborers Local 210, as a commonly known power base. However, within 20 years, it began to wane under a perfect storm of factors: the Mafia lost control of the laborers in the 1990s, younger generations did not follow their fathers into organized crime, state-sponsored gambling became common, and informants became even more common. It was thought that local pizzeria owner Joseph Todaro Sr. took over for Magaddino, with his son following him, but Todaro Jr. is quoted in Dan Herbeck's March 19, 2017, *Buffalo News* story as saying, "I'm not going to comment [on organized crime questions], but if you want a great recipe for cheese and pepperoni, I'll tell you."

Many local reporters have followed suspected Mafia figures in Buffalo for decades; searches of the *Buffalo News* and *Buffalo Courier-Express* archives turn up hundreds of stories. For book-length summaries, try *Gangsters and Organized Crime in Buffalo*, by Mike Rizzo, and *The Real Teflon Don*, by Matt Gryta and George Karalus.

WE DON'T SAY "BUFFALO WINGS" HERE

. . . but, regardless, how were wings really invented?

Manhattan-based food writer Arthur Bovino's carefully researched history of Buffalo's connection to the chicken wing starts in the 19th century; historic menus from as far back as 1857 list "chicken wings, fried" as part of their offerings, though these iterations would not be recognizable as what gets served in local pubs today. The story almost everyone in Buffalo knows is that, on a Friday night in 1964, Teressa Bellissimo, Anchor co-owner, had a carton of whole chicken wings she didn't know what to do with, and decided to halve them, fry them and dress them in a cayenne pepper sauce. Her son and his friends were the taste-testers and loved them. The accompanying celery and blue cheese dressing came later.

However, Arthur Bovino, author of *Buffalo Everything: A Guide to Eating in "The Nickel City,"* relates that there are different origin stories out there. One involves writer Calvin Trillin, who traveled to Buffalo in 1980 to do a story on wings for the New Yorker. Trillin talked to African American restaurateur John Young, who was serving breaded chicken wings with a hot "mombo" sauce from 1961 to 1970 (when he left Buffalo). Bovino also reports that, in Chicago, starting in 1950, a "mumbo" sauce was being served that may have made its way to Washington, DC, and then to John Young's attention in Buffalo, via travelers.

For exhaustive history, descriptions, and recommendations on Buffalo's best eating, there is an excellent source: Arthur Bovino's *Buffalo Everything: A Guide to Eating in "The Nickel City."*

THE COMPLEX ORIGIN OF CHICKEN WINGS

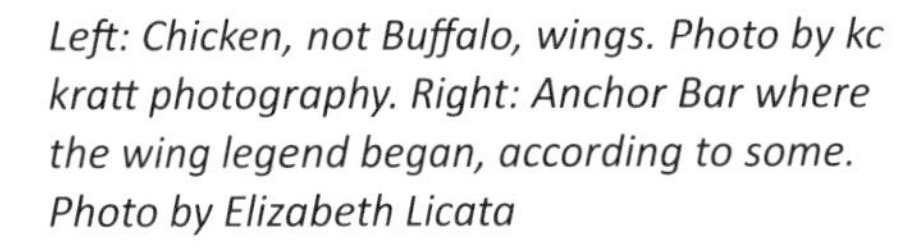

Left: Chicken, not Buffalo, wings. Photo by kc kratt photography. Right: Anchor Bar where the wing legend began, according to some. Photo by Elizabeth Licata

WHAT: A not-so-simple story

WHERE: Anchor Bar, Duffs, Bar-Bill, Nine-Eleven tavern, and many other WNY wing joints

COST: Varies

PRO TIP: Buy the Bovino book.

There are some who believe someone at the Anchor Bar may have experienced Young's battered and sauced wings and gotten inspired to create the version we know.

Finally, there is Frank's RedHot sauce, the cayenne-based sauce used at Anchor until the restaurant began to create and market its own. Anchor's use of this sauce was revealed in a *Buffalo Courier Express* story in the early 1970s, and the revelation has made cayenne pepper key to the "Buffalo" flavor that is now marketed in restaurants and supermarkets throughout the US. Sadly, many other ingredients, mostly in highly processed powdered forms, have been added to "Buffaloize" all sorts of foods. Buffalo wing soda, anyone? Buffalo cupcakes? Wing lovers in Buffalo just shake their heads and go for a medium order at Anchor Bar, Duff's, Bar Bill Tavern, Nine-Eleven Tavern, Gabriel's Gate, La Nova, Kelly's Korner, or any other well-regarded Western New York wing destination.

A MENTAL HOSPITAL THAT BECAME A DESTINATION

Will the stories behind this transformed landmark be lost?

Now known mainly as an architectural masterpiece by H. H. Richardson, Buffalo State Hospital's beautiful original Medina sandstone and brick buildings were designed in 1870 in the Kirkbride plan and took 23 years to complete. The Thomas Kirkbride plan of asylum design included a central administration area with expansive wings on either side; tall, airy rooms and maximum sunlight were priorities. Curved corridors were meant to discourage the practice of placing beds in these spaces, but as the years passed, the hospital became overcrowded, with Kirkbride's plan of peaceful, sanitary conditions for mental patients abandoned. New buildings were constructed in the late 1960s, and Richardson's structures fell into disuse.

New York State stepped up to provide funds for restoration and reuse of the older structures; the three central buildings—an iconic administrative structure with towers and two adjacent wards—have become a boutique hotel (Hotel Henry) and conference center/event space. Eventually, the remaining historic structures on either side also will find public uses as part of the Richardson Olmsted Campus. It

BUFFALO STATE HOSPITAL TOURS

WHAT: Finally, a chance to see what was off limits for decades

WHERE: 444 Forest Ave.

COST: $20–$40 per person

PRO TIP: These tours are offered only from May through September; see richardson-olmsted.com or more information.

Above: Inside view and close-up exterior view of Buffalo State Hospital, Buffalo, NY. Photos by kc kratt photography. Inset: The hospital, Buffalo, N.Y. circa 1900. Photo courtesy of the Detroit Publishing Company photograph collection, Library of Congress

is possible to take tours that include the undeveloped parts of the complex, providing a fascinating look at mental illness treatment in the 19th century.

Thought of for many years as abandoned, the original structures of the Buffalo State Hospital slowly are being brought back into reuse. What many do not realize is that much of the campus is still used for mental health purposes.

A TUCKED-AWAY MUSEUM

Where's the best place to learn about the company that made Buffalo?

Around the turn of the 20th century, a small soap factory became one of the country's leading mail-order businesses, thanks to the acumen of John Larkin. At the Larkin Company's peak, it sold a large variety of products to two million customers across America. As a side benefit, Larkin brought Frank Lloyd Wright to Buffalo; Wright designed homes for three top Larkin executives. The company declined after 1920 and by mid-century was all but defunct, but Buffalonians can enjoy a trip back in time to when "everybody worked for Larkin" by visiting a gallery devoted to Larkin history and memorabilia. It's located in the former Larkin B, C, D, D Annex, E, F, G, H, J, K, N, O building, a huge structure in Buffalo's hydraulics district (also called Larkinville), on the first floor. On view are Larkin soap products, paints, enamels, varnishes, razor strops, clothes wringers, home medicine kits, and much more, including drawings, books, and other printed matter relating to the company and those who ran it. Most of the material dates to the early 20th century. The gallery was founded

LARKIN GALLERY

WHAT: A treasure trove of memorabilia from one of Buffalo's most important companies

WHERE: 701 Seneca St.

COST: Free

PRO TIP: Pick up *Images of America: The Larkin Company* book.

John Larkin's brother-in-law, Elbert Hubbard, worked for Larkin before founding the Roycroft artisan community in East Aurora.

Left: John Larkin. Right: Making soap in the old factory. Photos courtesy of the Buffalo History Museum

by Larkin devotees Sharon Osgood, Jerry Puma, and Patrick Mahoney.

Though warehouse buildings remain from the heyday of the Larkin Soap Company—and most have been cleverly reused—the most famous Larkin structure, Frank Lloyd Wright's Larkin Administration Building (1906), one of the most innovative office buildings of its time, is no more. As Jack Quinan, a leading Wright scholar states, "The loss of the Larkin Building was a loss of staggering significance. Its loss is at least equivalent to losing one of Gaudi's major works in Barcelona. These buildings encapsulate an age; they are the highest artistic achievement of a civilization at a given time."

One brick pier remains on the site.

THE WILDEST CITY HALL IN THE US (page 50)
Photo by Steve Rosenthal

WOMEN OF THE PEN (page 170)
Photo of Jana Willoughby-Lohr by kc kratt photography

THE HOUSE THAT A PROPHECY BUILT (page 4)
Photo by kc kratt photography

A TRUE TALE OF 'WECK (page 114)
Photo by kc kratt photography

THIS IS ONLY A TEST (page 46)
Photo by Elizabeth Licata

A MID-CENTURY MODERN MECCA (page 150)
Photo by Elizabeth Licata

NATURE BATS LAST (page 186)
Photo by Elizabeth Licata

A REFUGE FOR RARE WATERFOWL (page 32)
Photo courtesy of Gooseneck Hill

A MAGICAL BACKROOM (page 74)
Photo by Stephen Gabris

A HIGH SCHOOL GYMNASIUM LOADED WITH HISTORY (page 56)
Photo by Stephen Gabris

A TINY SECRET GARDEN (page 108)
Photo by Don Zinteck/Photographics 2

THE SHED (page 112)
Photo by kc kratt photography

THE MIGHTY ZOAR (page 44)
Photo by Stephen Gabris

THE GORGE IS THE THING (page 42)
Photo by kc kratt photography

THE CHURCH THAT BECAME A LIVING SCULPTURE (page 172)
Photo by Elizabeth Licata

ART UNDERGROUND (page 2)
Photo by Elizabeth Licata

THE OTHER ST. PATRICK'S DAY PARADE

How does the most Irish part of Buffalo celebrate St. Patty's?

While Buffalo's massive Delaware Avenue St. Patrick's Day parade gets—by far—the biggest crowds, a few blocks to the south, another homegrown event is steadily attracting attendees and participants. The "Old Neighborhood" parade started in 1993, but its route echoes Buffalo's early 20th-century parades, which encompassed such Old First Ward streets as Chicago, Abbott, Hamburg, and O'Connell. In 1942, this parade moved to Delaware Avenue, downtown, where it is still the main St. Patrick's Day event, held the closest Sunday to March 17.

Buffalo's first media-documented St. Patrick's Day Parade (*Buffalo Morning Express*) was in 1848, though there may have been parades before this. It was held by members of the Friendly Sons of St. Patrick, a fraternal organization formed by established Irish immigrants to assist both new immigrants and their countrymen suffering in the Great Famine at home. The sequence of regular parades and revivals of discontinued parades is sporadic, but, sometime between 1913 and 1915, it was famously revived/started, depending on whose story is preferred. The final revival happened in 1935.

"OLD NEIGHBORHOOD" ST. PATRICK'S DAY PARADE

WHAT: A parade that retraces— to some degree— the original Buffalo event

WHERE: Starts at 93 Leddy St., at noon

COST: Free

PRO TIP: Get there early. Parking spots and vantage points disappear quickly.

Sights from the Old Neighborhood parade. Photos by kc kratt photography

The Old Neighborhood parade is held on the closest Saturday. It starts at Hamburg Street and finishes at South and Louisiana, winding through the narrow streets of the Old First Ward, where Buffalo's first Irish American settlers lived and worked, most of them either helping to build the Erie Canal or providing the labor needed to scoop grain from incoming freighters into the massive silos that still stand around Buffalo's Inner Harbor. The parade is organized by the Valley Community Center; its route highlights the historic churches of the neighborhood as well as the waterfront and other sites with deep resonance for Buffalo's Irish American community. The marchers and floats include union workers and neighborhood businesses, as well the usual bands and dancers. There is no need to argue about which parade is the most "authentic." Both parades have deep historic roots, and both should be experienced.

A big plus of the "Old Neighborhood Parade" is its proximity to some of Buffalo's most beloved taverns, such as Gene McCarthy's, Cook's, and Adolf's.

POLISH PASTRIES

Which seasonal treats are less fun to pronounce than eat?

Chrusciki (kroo-she-kee) and paczki (pounch-kee) are key Easter season indulgences in Buffalo. Chrusciki, crispy twisted pastries that are fried and then dusted with powdered sugar, generally are seen at Polish weddings and the weeks leading up to Easter. Paczki, rich jelly doughnuts filled with prune, raspberry, or lemon jam, become available on the Tuesday before Ash Wednesday (Fat Tuesday). For many Buffalonians, this is as close as we get to the bacchanalia of Mardi Gras: a rich, overstuffed doughnut, topped with powdered sugar. Paczki are offered year-round by a few venues. The origin of these is said to be based on Middle Ages–era cooks needing to get rid of sugar, eggs, lard, and fruit in advance of Lenten fasting.

Though not exclusive to Buffalo, the doughnuts are a longtime tradition.

POLISH PASTRIES

WHAT: Traditional specialties at their finest

WHERE: Two reliable go-tos are E. M. Chrusciki Bakery, 80 West Dullard Ave., in Lancaster, NY; and Mazurek's Bakery, 543 South Park Ave.

COST: $5–$10, depending on quantity

PRO TIP: The pastries are most commonly available in early spring.

Small, local bakeries struggle throughout the US, but Buffalo is lucky enough to support several longtime bakeries that specialize in ethnic, particularly Polish, specialties. These include chrusciki, paczki, kołaczki, placek, and others.

Paczki. Illustration by Jean-Pierre Thimot

As for placek, these are popular during the Christmas and Easter seasons (really, all year-round). The word simply means "cake" in Polish, but in Buffalo, placek refers to a sweet yeast bread topped with sugary crumble, with or without golden raisins. It can be found at both the bakeries mentioned here and at many others, even local supermarkets.

A TINY SECRET GARDEN

Can artistry and obsessive-compulsive disorder combine to create a miniature masterpiece?

While the spectacular home of Arlan Peters and Dominic DeFillippo is impressive in any season, the exterior is a compelling showplace in summer, thanks to its surrounding gardens. These are designed in a classic, traditional fashion, with colorful borders in front and quiet green expanses in back, complementing the architecture, as well as garden sculpture salvaged from a Buffalo estate and a shed designed and built by the homeowners.

Somewhat of a traffic jam is caused during Garden Walk Buffalo, when visitors stop along the walkway to view an intricate "moss garden" tucked away in a shady area alongside the house. This is not a traditional moss garden, but rather a miniature village, complete with a working water mill. The theme is bucolic, evoking a 19th-century rural English village. Everything is

ARLAN PETERS MOSS GARDEN

WHAT: A miniature handmade village within a garden

WHERE: 20 Norwood Ave.

COST: Free

PRO TIP: This can be seen only during Garden Walk Buffalo, held on the last full weekend of July. Saturday morning and early afternoon are likely the least-busiest times.

Buffalo gardening is now defined by a book, *Buffalo-Style Gardens*, by Sally Cunningham and Jim Charlier. It features some of the most well-known properties in Garden Walk Buffalo, billed as America's largest garden tour, as well as beautiful suburban gardens.

A miniature garden makes a big impact. Photo by Don Zinteck

tiny—and perfect. If it's a sunny day, the owners will also bring out a perfect replica of their house, complete with gardens, featuring equally meticulous craftsmanship.

It's important to note that Peters was a longtime president of the Garden Walk effort, a volunteer position. A self-taught master craftsman, Peters also has been active in the restoration of Shea's Performing Arts Center and Frank Lloyd Wright's Martin House, and recently he built a miniature replica of the tragically demolished Wright-designed Larkin Administration building. No tour of Garden Walk Buffalo is complete without a viewing of the Peters moss garden, even if it means standing in line to see it.

A SPECTACULAR CREEKSIDE RETREAT

What happens when a British hosta expert and an American daylily pro get together?

Those who make the extra effort to find this expansive and impressive private garden can go away knowing they've seen one of Western New York's best. The garden is only available for viewing during Fridays in July. Mike and Kathy Shadrack took over the property of a former Buffalo Bills player and transformed it into—yes—a showplace, but a showplace with subtlety. To begin with, the house and adjacent deck are built over a tree-lined creek, with expansive terraced gardens surrounding the house. Sunny areas feature bright beds of daylilies, iris, spring bulbs, and flowering shrubs, while shaded areas highlight a variety of hostas—more than 1,000—including many rare cultivars, as well as other shade perennials.

Smug Creek Gardens also features obelisks, sculptures, and less definable types of garden art. Almost every plant is labeled. The Shadracks are well known to garden professionals throughout the US, but much less so in Western New York. With the advent of the Open Gardens program, however, it's possible for local enthusiasts to visit a space previously familiar only to in-the-know plant specialists. In addition to Open Gardens,

SMUG CREEK GARDENS

WHAT: A spectacular Creekside garden

WHERE: Hamburg, NY

COST: Free

PRO TIP: Smug Creek is open to the public on Friday afternoons in July, as part of the Open Gardens program. Visit gardensbuffaloniagara.com for more information.

A garden with a rainbow of daylilies. Photo by Elizabeth Licata

the Shadracks sometimes host special events at their property, occasionally serving high tea as a nod to Mike's 40 years as an English bobby before he moved to the US and married Kathy. It's just as much fun to spend time with this charming couple as it is to tour their gardens.

Mike and Kathy Shadrack have written several well-regarded gardening titles between them, including *The New Encyclopedia of Hostas* and *The Book of Little Hostas*. Examples of their expertise can be seen throughout their Southtowns property.

THE SHED

Is there anyone who does not know about Garden Walk's worst-kept secret?

Check out the most Instagrammable garden shed ever during the next Garden Walk Buffalo. A talented designer, longtime Garden Walk participant Jim Charlier, is always ready for a new project. In late 2014, he decided he needed a shed to hold gardening supplies that were taking up too much space in his garage. There was never any question of buying a prefab structure or kit; Charlier decided early on that the shed would echo the historic architecture of his 1897 Dutch Colonial Revival house.

As it progressed, he added many more embellishments, and the interior of the shed includes artworks, custom shelving, Caesarstone countertops, and a wide range of decor, including tiki heads, boat oars, and porcelain hands. The shed's doors, windows, and paneling, as well as other elements, are all repurposed. What now is known as Taj-ma-shed

TAJ-MA-SHED

WHAT: A graphic designer's interpretation of a utility shed

WHERE: 215 Lancaster Ave.

COST: Free, during July Open Gardens, held every Friday in July; and Garden Walk Buffalo, held the last weekend of July

PRO TIP: Check out the Charlier garden, including the shed, during Open Gardens; these self-guided tours are much less crowded than the big event.

Jim Charlier is largely responsible for changing Garden Walk from a secret to a national bucket list garden tour. He created the GW logo, masterminded a PR strategy, and contributed to two books that focus on Buffalo gardens.

The shed turned into a work of art.
Photos by kc kratt photography

was completed in the summer of 2016 and became an instant hit, with comprehensive coverage from print publications *This Old House* and *Buffalo Spree*, as well as dozens of online hits. Because it can be seen only during July, during Open Gardens, and Garden Walk Buffalo, it's still fair to consider the Charlier shed a secret—of sorts!

A TRUE TALE OF 'WECK

Does it matter how they spell it?

One of America's most unknown sandwiches is a Buffalo standard, with versions of various quality levels available everywhere in the region. Several local eateries use beef on 'weck as their marquee attraction, offering standout examples. But how did this sandwich of thin-sliced roast beef in a salted, caraway-studded bun get started? The details are hazy.

Longtime Buffalo reporter and historian Steve Cichon traces it to the 1901 Pan-American Exposition, at which time tavern owner Joseph Gohn fed hungry tourists with roasted beef sandwiches from his location on Delaware Avenue and West Delevan Street. The rolls are attributed to German immigrant William Wahr, who ran a bakery on Buffalo's East Side from 1891 to 1924. These rolls, variously called kimmelweck, kummelweck, or just 'weck, are largely what give the sandwich its character. The main point of this research is that, while Buffalo may be famous for wings, beef on 'weck is an equally significant claim to culinary fame. Some might even say it has a better claim.

"You bite into the soft, squishy bun and get hit by fruity caraway and the abrasive sharpness of pretzel salt that seems like it's going to be too much until a fraction of a second later when the thin, still-rare layers of beef flood your mouth with bronzed, unsweetened, underseasoned, caramel notes . . . Think beef on 'weck as a lesson in sandwich masochism."
—Arthur Bovino, *Buffalo Everything*

A 'weck sandwich. Photo by kc kratt photography

Whereas nobody really thinks much about the quality of the chicken in chicken wings, the beef that goes into beef on 'weck is another matter. Arthur Bovino delved into this issue and reports that Buffalo's Charlie the Butcher swears by top round, which he says is the "single leanest muscle, but we tenderize and age it overnight." The key for all places serving this iconic sandwich is that it must be sliced thin.

BEEF ON 'WECK

WHAT: Buffalo's lesser-known specialty

WHERE: Four inarguable go-tos are Schwabl's, 789 Center Rd., West Seneca, NY; Eckl's, 703 Seneca St., Buffalo, NY; Bar-Bill Tavern, 185 Main St., East Aurora, NY; and Charlie the Butcher, 1065 Wehrle Dr., Williamsville, NY (with other locations). There are many others.

COST: Usually under $10

PRO TIP: Look for venues where the beef is carved in full view of diners.

YOU LOVE THE ARCHITECTURE; NOW CHECK OUT THE FLOWERS

Want to see a Frank Lloyd Wright-designed garden?

It took decades to fully restore Frank Lloyd Wright's magnificent Martin House campus (1903–09), which includes the Darwin Martin house, a pergola, a conservatory, the Barton house, and a gardener's cottage. A visitor's center, designed by Toshiko Mori, was added in 2009. The final step in the restoration process was the historic landscape, completed in 2019. Now, instead of a bland expanse of lawn, the house is surrounded by interesting plantings, including, most famously, a "Floricycle." At first called a "Hemicycle," this semicircular planting contains 12 repeated plantings of perennials and bulbs, designed for spring into fall bloom and backed up by shrubs. It provides a lively, colorful frame for an architectural masterpiece, and deserves its own tour.

MARTIN HOUSE CAMPUS LANDSCAPING

WHAT: The garden Wright designed, finally recreated

WHERE: 125 Jewett Pkwy.

COST: Free, unless an interior tour is included

PRO TIP: See this post-2021, when the "sleep, creep, leap" sequence will have been completed.

Wright worked with fellow architect Walter Burley Griffin, who later became known for his work in Australia, and, very intensively, with his clients Darwin and Isabelle Martin, who were insistent on extensive gardens and suggested additions and alterations

Colorful flower gardens designed by Wright. Photos by Elizabeth Licata

throughout the process. Then, they maintained the landscape for more than 30 years. Black-and-white images of it show lush, mature plantings, with the shrubs easily as tall as Isabelle Martin. The Floricycle, planned to provide horticultural interest from March through November (very realistic for Buffalo), starts with snowdrops and ends with asters and mums.

Not all Wright's clients went along with his landscaping ideas. In the case of Isabelle and Darwin Martin, the clients responsible for Buffalo's magnificent Martin House campus, the Martins insisted on a more expansive landscape than Wright had planned and worked with the architect every step of the way, editing closely every design and every list of plants.

A DISTRICT NAMED FOR A DOG BISCUIT

What's Buffalo's most recognizable, but least understood, industrial area?

Buffalo's East Side is a mystery to many residents. Too often, it is lumped together as though a homogenous neighborhood, when in fact it is filled with separate and fascinating historic enclaves, many filled with interesting architecture.

Not far from Main Street, just northeast of the Frederick Law Olmsted-designed Martin Luther King Park, lies the Milk-Bone dog biscuit factory, which is still operational. Founded in New York City in 1908, Milk-Bone outgrew its factory there in 1957 and moved to Buffalo. The blocks that surround it contain the original buildings for many other iconic brands, including the National Biscuit Company, Val Duttenhofer Sons, General Electric Company, George Urban Milling Company, Continental Baking Company, and others. Some of the companies fed generations of Buffalo workers. The historic sites, though many

MILK-BONE DISTRICT

WHAT: Start at Milk-Bone plant, 216 Fougeron St.

WHERE: A lesser-known industrial district

COST: Free, self-guided walking tour

PRO TIP: Check Facebook for Buffalo Belt Line; it hosts a guided tour every May.

Many of America's most iconic brands got their start in Buffalo. Though the manufacturing may have moved elsewhere, the buildings and the history remain.

Milk-Bone dog biscuit factory. Photo by Elizabeth Licata

are unoccupied, are still well worth viewing for their own sake by architecture/history buffs. Economic development types hope that the structures will soon be redeveloped for job creation.

According to urbanist and historian Chris Hawley, who also works for the city of Buffalo, “The Milk-Bone District is a place where labor created value through globally known products like Wonder Bread, Hostess Cakes, and Milk-Bone dog treats. The buildings where these products were made are still here, and they tell a great story.”

GARDENVILLE IS REAL

Why do people who have barely heard of him flock to the longtime hometown of Charles Burchfield?

In Burchfield's day, Gardenville was a rural enclave in the town of West Seneca, a suburb of Buffalo. The artist lived here from 1925 until his death in 1967. The town provided a refuge for his large family and a place where he could have a quiet studio, close to nature. Here is where the artist did many of his large, hallucinatory renditions of nature captured in swirling strokes, heightened colors, and exaggerated forms.

Now, decades after Burchfield's death, Western New Yorkers flock to Gardenville, and the rest of West Seneca, to buy plants and plan their summer gardens. Though many of them have no knowledge of Burchfield's love for Western New York wildflowers such as hepatica and native columbines, they are searching out equally precious blooms among the

GARDENVILLE

WHAT: A district devoted to nurseries

WHERE: Throughout West Seneca, NY

COST: Browsing is free, but flowers have price tags.

PRO TIP: Some of these nurseries are seasonal; the best time to visit is in early summer.

Charles E. Burchfield's Gardenville Studio is recreated within the Burchfield Penney Art Center as a permanent installation. Visitors can see his working method, the shelves he used to store his drawings, and the objects that inspired him, including a stuffed snowy owl.

Garden path. Photo by Elizabeth Licata

area's many family-owned greenhouses and garden centers. While many other regions of the US much depend on big-box hardware monoliths for gardening needs, Buffalo has the advantage of a destination named for some its most desirable consumer assets.

FROM ZAGREB TO BUFFALO

Where does a shot of slivovitz have special meaning?

The Croatian Club was founded in 1923 to serve the Croatian population of Buffalo's northwest enclaves of Riverside and Black Rock. Originally, the building was to have additional floors built on top of the "dugout," but a lack of funds during the Depression halted expansion, and the club remains an underground spot.

During the early 1960s, the club was frequented by Buffalo Bills coach Lou Saban, who was of Croatian descent. But there is a certain éclat surrounding the "Cro Club" that makes it attractive to all ethnicities.

Originally the building was to have additional floors built on top of the "dugout," but a lack of funds during the Depression

THE CRO CLUB

WHAT: A haven for Croatian Americans

WHERE: 226 Condon Ave.

COST: Price of a drink

PRO TIP: Call ahead before visiting in case a private event is in progress, or, better yet, book a tour through ForgottenBuffalo.com.

Croatians began to settle in Buffalo in the early 20th century; many left their country, which was soon to transition into Yugoslavia, for mostly economic reasons. Many worked in Buffalo's shipyards and factories. They founded churches and kept their homegrown traditions alive. Some eventually returned to Croatia.

The Croatian Club dates back to 1923. Photo by Elizabeth Licata

halted expansion. For more than 40 years, the club was home to the legendary bartender Bob Svetko who befriended many Buffalo politicians, including Mayor Jimmy Griffin.

NAMED AFTER A POET/ ACTIVIST

Is this the second most Polish place in Buffalo?

The first most Polish place is generally agreed to be St. Stanislaus Church, an institution with a history inextricably connected to Buffalo's Polish American community. But, after the religious institutions, there are countless other organizations that have supported Buffalo's Polish American community from its earliest years.

The Adam Mickiewicz Library and Dramatic Circle, founded in 1895, is the oldest Polish American organization and oldest Polish library in Western New York. It's named after Adam Mickiewicz (1798-1855), who was a Polish poet, dramatist, essayist, publicist, translator, professor of Slavic literature, and political activist. He is among three such figures designated as a "Polish Bard." In addition to its 12,000-volume library, the bar here serves more than 50 different imported beers, with a large Polish selection. "Adam Mickey's" also has been home to most of Torn Space Theater's productions and a large annual Dyngus Day party, as well as other cultural events.

The Dyngus Day activities at Adam Mickey's include authentic polka music and dancing, a popular buffet, a Polish beer bar, and the famous Buffalo's Best Kielbasa Contest. Categories include Homemade, Commercial, Wholesale Kielbasa, and People's Choice.

THE ADAM MICKIEWICZ LIBRARY AND DRAMATIC CIRCLE

WHAT: A pillar of Polonia

WHERE: 612 Fillmore Ave.

COST: Depends on whether you're having a drink or seeing a play

PRO TIP: This is the site of a serious kielbasa contest every Dyngus Day.

Left: Adam Mickiewicz Library & Dramatic Circle. Photo by kc kratt photography.
Right: Adam Mickiewicz bar.

Recently, Torn Space Theater, which uses the Adam Mickiewicz theater for its productions, has undertaken the restoration of the Adam Mickiewicz exterior as well as the transformation of an adjacent gas mart into a 1,545-square-foot design studio, green room, and conference facility. The importance of this East Side landmark as a cultural center has been reinforced and reinvigorated in the process.

Poles began to arrive in Buffalo in the 1850s and 1860s; many were escaping political oppression and poverty in Germany, Austria, and Russia, as there was no formal nation of Poland at that time. It had been partitioned between the three countries in 1772.

WHERE TO FIND THEM ALL

Want to take a trip on Buffalo's Polonia Trail?

A day spent touring some of Buffalo's most iconic Polish American landmarks is a day spent enjoying architectural beauty and a rich ethnic culture. It's possible to create a DIY tour, but the Polonia Trail website has downloadable maps for self-guided tours of Polish American locations throughout Buffalo. Churches, cultural centers, Polish American–owned businesses, and more are on the navigable trail. Part of The Polish Legacy Project and founded by two Western New York Polish Americans (James Lawicki and Andrzej Golebiowski), the website features links to groups and historical stories on the trail. In addition to the more well-known sites, others include Buffalo Bathhouse No. 2, Dom Polski North Tonawanda, the Holy Mother of the Rosary Polish National Church Complex in Lancaster, and many other fascinating landmarks.

POLONIATRAIL.COM

WHAT: A self-guided tour through Polish Buffalo

WHERE: poloniatrail.com

COST: Free with gas money

PRO TIP: Read carefully before visiting, as some of these sites have been razed. The history remains worth knowing.

Thanks to this website, anyone can physically or virtually explore architecture, clubs, meetinghouses, churches, cemeteries, and places that figured prominently in the growth of Western New York's Polonia.

Polonia Trail tours.

The Polonia Trail was inspired by Boston's Freedom Trail, which highlights sites of relevance to the American Revolution. It is supprted by the Polish American Congress, which has been serving American Polonia since 1944. One of this organization's most interesting statements is its "commitment to just and compassionate immigration policy in keeping with America's best traditions."

A SUB FOR THE AGES

Who could resist this simple but ingenious Buffalo sandwich?

A lesser-known Buffalo culinary invention has been a late-night staple for twentysomethings for decades. The chicken finger sub was created by the chef/owners of John's Pizza & Subs in 1982. The sandwich gradually evolved from a chicken Parmesan concept and a memory of a local "chicken plank" sandwich that was based on a fish fry but with chicken and shaken with hot sauce. It seemed natural to put the chicken in a sub roll with blue cheese.

As one of the inventors, Gene Mongan, who still works at John's, says, "Blue cheese and hot sauce, put those things together—you can make a cake and put frosting on it and people would eat it. It's just a great combination."

CHICKEN FINGER SUB

WHAT: Chicken wings without the bones but with all the flavors

WHERE: Try the original at John's Pizza and Subs. But variations are offered througout Western New York and Western Pennsylvania.

COST: About $10 at John's Pizza & Subs, where it is available also as a pizza and as a platter

PRO TIP: Avoid the big chains, where subs may not be freshly made and ingredients could be subpar.

Christa Seychew, Buffalo food historian and critic: "The chicken finger sub is such a basic concept. And yet, it appears to be available only in Western New York. (Ask expatriates, and they'll confirm this.) Some might consider it our Philly cheesesteak, but with a key difference—this one hasn't gone national, except in bastardized form."

Top: Chicken finger sub. Photo by kc kratt photography. Inset: John's Pizza & Subs, origin of the chicken finger sub. Photo by Elizabeth Licata

A PLACE FOR EVERYONE

Is this one of Buffalo's most interesting melting pots?

The original owner of this 1866 mansion was Cicero J. Hamlin, a wealthy sugar investor. Hamlin was the first president of American Glucose Company, which employed more than 1,000. The company began as Buffalo Grape Sugar Company—glucose manufacturing was an important industry in 19th-century Buffalo—and later was the American Grape Sugar Company until it was consolidated with several Midwest companies. Hamlin also was known for the Village Stock Farm in the town of Aurora. He bred 500 cattle each year, maintained an extensive stock of fine thoroughbred stallions and mares, and had a driving park east of Main Street that was developed with housing around the turn of the 20th century and now is known as the Hamlin Park Historic District.

TROOP I/HAMLIN HOUSE

WHAT: A friendly drinking hole and event center for a diverse neighborhood

WHERE: 432 Franklin St.

COST: Price of a drink on up

PRO TIP: See if a staffer can give you a tour of the upper floors.

Famous Hamlin descendants include Chauncey Hamlin (1881-1963), a benefactor of the Buffalo Museum of Science; painter Martha Visser't Hooft (1906-1994); and actor Harry Hamlin (born 1951), best known for his roles in *L. A. Law* and *Clash of the Titans*. Cicero Hamlin's home at 432 Franklin St. is one of a handful of Italian villas built of solid brick in Buffalo, characterized by low-pitched, hip roofs; decorative elliptical windows; and a three-story tower on the left side of the structure. The family left this house in 1886; it was occupied subsequently by the German Singing Society and purchased by the American Legion Troop I Post 665 in 1939. Other organizations

Left: Troop I/Hamlin House. Below: Interior detail. Photos by Nancy J. Parisi

have long been welcome in the large structure, including many local neighborhood groups. Troop I/Hamlin House is renowned for its Friday fish fries. The bar is run by the American Legion Post.

A 19th-century structure that served briefly as a city mansion for one of Buffalo's most interesting industrial barons has evolved over the years and ended up as a headquarters for the American Legion Post 665, as well as a haven for its neighborhood's LGBTQ community and a friendly, affordable venue for events of all descriptions.

HATMAKER TO HOLLYWOOD

Where does HBO look for period-perfect headgear?

Gary White's work has been seen on some of the most famous heads in the world. Remember the yellow beaver fedoras worn by Warren Beatty in the movie *Dick Tracy*? Val Kilmer and Kurt Russell's headgear in *Tombstone*? Hats worn by actors in HBO's *Boardwalk Empire*, Martin Scorsese's *The Irishman*, and the film *Marshall*, shot in Buffalo, all have Custom Hatter labels inside.

White, born Gary Witkowski, began as a stock boy and later hat buyer for local men's store Peller & Mure, and traveled to Lynn, Massachusetts, to learn the hat-making craft from the late Henry Goldstein. He opened the doors to the Custom Hatter in 1989.

White estimates that he makes from 500 to 1,000 hats annually; half of his customers are local, while the rest come from around the globe. The Custom Hatter offers 140 styles, including 60 Western versions, with price tags beginning in the $500–$600 range.

THE CUSTOM HATTER

WHAT: Handmade hats, often made for films

WHERE: 1318 Broadway

COST: The sky's the limit

PRO TIP: Those interested in the ultimate headwear shouldn't wait; White thinks of retiring and has no successor in mind.

"There is something about the mystique of the hat. It finishes off your wardrobe. It tells you something about the personality of a person. When someone puts a hat on, you finish the whole outfit right off and you make a statement by wearing the hat."—Gary White, the Custom Hatter

Hats from the Custom Hatter had an extra flair. Photo by kc kratt photography

Using archival tools and machinery, White starts with hat blocks of Appalachian yellow poplar; a flange machine helps form brims when high-pressure steam from irons is applied to the fur felt. Pouncing—sanding and smoothing of the finish of a hat—is accomplished by machine and hand, using fine powders, while leather sweatbands and bridal satin linings are imported from Italy. White has a collection of more than 300 different grosgrain ribbons, used as final touches.

THE BUFFALO SOUND

What drives Buffalo's powerful hip-hop scene?

It's not Los Angeles or Atlanta, but Buffalo has made a bigger impact on the hip-hop world nationwide than many know. Buffalo hip-hop got its big break thanks to the Griselda Records crew, a group of loosely connected artists, some of whom are still local and others who have moved on to national fame. Of these, Westside Gunn (Alvin Lamar Worthy), with his half-brother Conway the Machine (Demond Price), were the first Buffalo rappers to sign with a major label (in 2017). Westside Gunn's cousin, Benny the Butcher (Jeremie Pennick) is also a frequent collaborator.

While it's currently fashionable to speak of Buffalo's "renaissance," in an interview that aired on National Public Radio, Westside Gunn had this to say about his hometown: "Buffalo is very dusty. All the other cities evolved. Buffalo has just been diminishing since then. It was already bad then so just imagine now. Nothing in the East Side or West Side shows promise—it's just like, 'This is what we used to. This what it is. This is life." In the same interview, Conway the Machine adds, "You know what I'm saying? It's never really sunny, and I think our music reflects those type of feelings, of despair and just hopelessness."

There are many Buffalonians who might not agree with this appraisal, but they'd need to understand that there are many Buffalos and many ways of growing up in Buffalo.

> "Westside Gunn, Conway the Machine, and Benny the Butcher are what some call your favorite rapper's favorite rappers—a title that implies that beyond the charts and the awards there's a more meaningful ranking system."
> —Frannie Kelley, National Public Radio

YouTube screenshot, Griselda explores Buffalo

BUFFALO HIP-HOP

WHAT: A scene that evolved on Buffalo's meanest streets

WHERE: Follow @artdealer on Instagram.

COST: Most online listening is free.

PRO TIP: There is plenty of diversity here; not all Buffalo artists follow the gritty road of Westside Gunn. Live band-based, multi-genre, mash-ups also can be found, including intriguing jazz/hip-hop fusion work.

In a September 2020 piece, *Buffalo News* critic Jeff Miers notes that the Griselda sound has "a grittiness, an unabashed honesty, a clear love for classic, old-school hip-hop sounds, in-your-face vitality, and a commitment to wordy, virtuosic rapping."

With the Griselda marquee artists moving on to national fame, a vibrant group of artists remain, among them the Art Dealer collective, which includes ToneyBoi, Camo Monk, Brett Deneve, and Jae Skeese. Just as the early Hallwalls Contemporary Arts Center artists exploded on the national arts scene in the 1980s, edgy Buffalo hip-hop is making an impact that will be felt for decades to come.

WHERE A TIGHT ETHNIC COMMUNITY GATHERED

What is a Polish Home?

In 1906, Polish American architect Władysław H. Zawadzki built a Renaissance-style, four-story red brick building with a facade of Indiana limestone. It housed two stores, meeting rooms, a bowling alley, a billiard room, smoking lounges for men and women, and offices, as well as enough space for the 10,000 volumes of the Czytelnia Polska, the Polish Literary Association's library. It also enclosed a 4,000-square-foot auditorium with a 24-foot stage. Throughout the years, this space hosted the Dom Polski Association, Paderewski Singing Society, Polish Ladies Relief Committee, Polish National Alliance, and Polish Boy Scouts.

Buffalo's first Dom Polski is now the Matt Urban Center, a multifaceted human service organization that operates eight sites. Its namesake, Lt. Col. Matt

DOM POLSKI HOME/ MATT URBAN CENTER

WHAT: Buffalo's most distinctive Polish Home, or meeting hall

WHERE: 1081 Broadway St.

COST: Free to walk in and look around

PRO TIP: Go with forgottenbuffalo.com for tours of more local Dom Polskis, though many are closed. This is only the first.

Another Dom Polski, in North Tonawanda, is still operating as a "historic social and cultural club dedicated to the celebration and promotion of Polish culture in Buffalo."

Postcard showing the Dom Polski auditorium. Photo courtesy of the Buffalo History Museum

Urban was born in 1919, in Buffalo, of Polish immigrants, raised at 1153 Broadway, and attended School #57. He entered the US Army in 1941, serving as a captain with the 2nd Battalion (60th Regiment, 9th Infantry Division) in France during World War II. He received 28 decorations, including the Silver Star, Bronze Star, and Purple Heart. In 1980, he was awarded the Congressional Medal of Honor. President Jimmy Carter described Urban as the "Greatest Soldier in American History."

PUTTING THE CAMP INTO CAMPGROUND

You've heard of Jones Beach, but how about Jones Pond?

Expect weekend themes such as Cowboy, Bear Country, Friends & Family, and Mardi Gras at a well-kept gay campground, Jones Pond Campground and RV Park. The property was settled in 1829 by the Peter Jones family; their farmhouse, built in 1840, still stands. The pond was dug in 1885 under the supervision of John Jones, who owned the property until 1941. His descendants converted the site into a campground in 1963, adding a pool and a snack bar, but when they retired, the property declined.

Then, in 1991, two gay men, Robert Stone and Bill Cassavaugh, purchased Jones Pond with a vision of converting it to an all-male gay campground. The property had its ups and downs over the years, but new owners continued to come on board, improving the facilities and remaining true to the Jones Pond mission: creating a unique and welcoming environment for gay men.

Current owners Bryan Schafer and Matt McCormick say, "Our first impression of Jones Pond was the beauty of the property, full of trees, hills, water, and wonderful people." There are thousands of reservations made each season, counting repeat visitors and first-timers, and the property is one of the biggest contributors to its rural economy, just 90 minutes southeast of Buffalo.

JONES POND

WHAT: A distinctive gay campground

WHERE: 9835 Old State Rd., Angelica, NY

COST: Check the website for details.

PRO TIP: This isn't really a tourist spot.

A beautiful, welcoming property and campground. Photo courtesy of Jones Pond

Owner Bryan Schaefer says, “We are one of the biggest contributors to the local economy and we have excellent relations within our community and vendors. As new owners, we’ve made an effort to go around and to introduce ourselves to local businesses, including the sheriff’s department, local restaurants, the local bank, and, of course, our favorite local lumber company—I seem to be there every single day.” The Pond holds fundraisers for such groups as the local volunteer fire department, the Allegany Cancer Society, and Camp Good Days.

THE ART OF SAVING ART

Who do you call when a painting seems beyond hope?

Barely known in its own city, Buffalo State College's Art Conservation Department, founded in 1970 and brought to Buffalo State College from the State University of New York at Oneonta in 1987, is famous throughout North America and the world. In 2020, the Patricia H. and Richard E. Garman Art Conservation Department at Buffalo State College, one of only four such programs in the US, celebrated its 50th anniversary. During those 50 years, the department expertly conserved and restored thousands of objects, including a 15th-century marble statue from the Metropolitan Museum of Art, which had been broken into hundreds of pieces; 19 paintings from the Baroque and Reformation eras from a Pennsylvania museum; and the model used for the Starship Enterprise, used in 79 Star Trek

BUFFALO STATE COLLEGE ART CONSERVATION DEPARTMENT

WHAT: A place where art is saved and art conservators trained

WHERE: 1300 Elmwood Ave.

COST: Free open houses are held regularly for the public.

PRO TIP: Conservation clinics are usually held in September; members of the public can bring in artifacts by appointment.

The conservation of art is both a science and an art. As an art, it requires intuition; as a science, it involves laboratory-style technological knowledge and experience. All objects are treated on an individual basis. Conservation is not a craft, but a profession.

Conservation efforts at Buffalo State College. Photos by Jessica Kourkounis

episodes from 1966 to 1969, and now housed in the Smithsonian National Air and Space Museum.

Despite the popularity of conservation studies, there are only four master's degree programs in North America today, including those at New York University (the first), the University of Delaware, and Buffalo State. Course material for Buffalo's three-year program covers almost every kind of expertise—from old master prints to ancient baskets to Victorian jewelry chests. Almost the only area of cultural property that the program doesn't much cover is architecture, although students can go on to study architectural conservation elsewhere.

WHEN HE WAS JUST AN EDITOR

Where can you find the last vestige of Mark Twain?

Mark Twain lived here in Buffalo 18 months (August, 1869, to March, 1871), just long enough to experience married life for the first time, serve as a newspaper editor for the last time, own his first home, and suffer a series of personal hardships. It is for this reason that most Twain historians write off his Buffalo years as a brief and unhappy blip that the author was eager to put behind him.

However, Twain scholar Thomas J. Reigstad's *Scribblin' for a Livin'* provides an in-depth look at Twain in Buffalo, including his tenure as editor and co-owner of the *Buffalo Express*. The most fascinating anecdotes surround Twain's work at the *Buffalo Express*.

Surrounded by cigar smoke, grime, and the pervasive smell of printers' ink, Twain's methodology for "waking up journalism in Buffalo" included introducing whimsy and comedic flair to police court reports, carefully choosing and embellishing bizarre news items, and producing exaggerated and viciously satiric "reports."

MARK TWAIN'S CARRIAGE HOUSE

WHAT: The last vestige of the author's Buffalo abode

WHERE: Delaware Avenue and Virginia Street

COST: Free, but almost impossible to see

PRO TIP: This is private property, but since it is mainly a parking lot, a quick peek is not a problem.

Brief though his time here was, Twain's time in Buffalo is a story worth telling.

Above: The Carriage House. Photo by Elizabeth Licata.
Inset: Scribblin' for a Livin' *tells the tale of Twain's time in Buffalo.*

There is one physical reminder of Twain's time here. At the northwest corner of Delaware Avenue and Virginia Street, where Twain's Buffalo residence once stood—it was destroyed by fire in 1963—the mansion's carriage house remains, set back on the Holloway Alley side of the property. Unfortunately, it is almost fully obscured by a three-story office/apartment complex.

A POSTHUMOUS STRUCTURE FOR THE DEAD

Could death stop Frank Lloyd Wright?

Never completed in Wright's lifetime, the Blue Sky Mausoleum was intended to be the final resting place of Wright's longtime friend, Darwin Martin, for whom he had designed a residential complex, a summer home, and a company headquarters. Designed between 1925 and 1928, this was never built, thanks to the Depression and Darwin Martin's failing business. In 2004, the plans were resurrected, and, after careful research, Forest Lawn Cemetery built the white granite and concrete memorial. The two rows of 12 crypts are low to the ground and gradually ascend to a small plaza, with a set of stairs between the rows. The memorial is unlike almost every other in Forest Lawn, dominated as it is by soaring obelisks and traditional funerary statuary. As was meant, the white stone dazzles against a blue sky on the right day.

BLUE SKY MAUSOLEUM

WHAT: A Frank Lloyd Wright design that was never built during his lifetime

WHERE: 1411 Delaware Ave.

COST: Free if self-guided; organized tours of the cemetery are ticketed.

PRO TIP: Go on a sunny day in summer to see the white stone dazzle.

The 24 crypts in this mausoleum represent the only opportunities in the world for one to choose to be memorialized in a structure designed by Frank Lloyd Wright.

Blue Sky Mausoleum designed by Frank Lloyd Wright. Photo courtesy of Forest Lawn Cemetery

How could Blue Sky be constructed after all this time? As with many of the architect's papers, Wright's drawings, notes and correspondence about Blue Sky were preserved, and, in 2004, Forest Lawn built it with the help of Anthony Puttnam, a one-time apprentice to Wright. The plans for Blue Sky were retired at the project's completion, which means that the design used to construct the memorial can't be used again.

A DISCO-ERA PIONEER CONTINUES TO EVOLVE

What do *Saturday Night Fever* and the Museum of Modern Art have in common?

Founded in Buffalo in 1975 by Paul Gregory and Rick Spaulding, Litelab's initial claim to fame was its work for disco clubs, including, most famously, the multicolored dance floor that appeared in *Saturday Night Fever*. The company pivoted quickly when disco waned in popularity, and it became known for its museum and high-end retail lighting. Litelab lighting can be found in the Metropolitan Museum of Art, the Wadsworth Atheneum, the Denver Museum of Art, Hirshhorn Museum, Musée du Luxembourg, and many, many other such institutions, as well as in banks, international corporate headquarters, libraries, and exclusive boutiques. The company specializes in museum-quality LED and replacement LED luminaires and operates globally, with participating factories on three

LITELAB CORPORATION

WHAT: Buffalo's internationally known lighting manufacturer

WHERE: 251 Elm St.

COST: The price of admission to one of the many museums Litelab has outfitted

PRO TIP: When lighting is important, this is the company to contact.

Litelab has received numerous awards and recognition from the American Institute of Architects and the International Association of Lighting Designers for its lighting products and fixtures.

The original Saturday Night Fever dance floor, as used in an Albright-Knox benefit. Photo courtesy of Albright-Knox Art Gallery

continents. All this originates from an understated, 19th-century industrial building on Buffalo's East Side.

While many of us tend to take lighting for granted—we just flip a switch so that rooms and objects can be visible—for nearly 50 years, Litelab has been studying the art and technology of lighting. Litelab is the very definition of a behind-the-scenes player, renowned among architects and architectural journals, but virtually unknown to the general public. Nonetheless, the work of Litelab is essential to our appreciation of many major public institutions—not to mention our appreciation of John Travolta in *Saturday Night Fever*.

THE LAST REFUGE

Is this secret club still in operation?

In 1926, a group of elite Buffalonians, upset that their private mens' enclave, the Saturn Club, had decided to crack down on club members' notorious Prohibition-era guzzling, decided to form a club that would be hidden from local law enforcement and Saturn Club disapproval.

They formed the Pack Corp., and purchased a very modest house in Allentown to house a new, ultra-exclusive social group. Membership is limited to 52 (hence the term "pack") at any time, and turnover is slow.

The Pack was granted tax-exempt status as a social club in 1941. Nobody will admit to belonging to this club, but reliable word has it that some of Buffalo's most recognizable names can be found on the roster, if there is one.

A 2013 *Buffalo Spree* story by Kevin Purdy featured quotes like this: "I'm not authorized to [speak on] that, and I don't know who's in charge there."

Purdy did have some interesting follow-up after that story. A 1970s-era Club bartender

THE PACK CLUB

WHAT: A tiny, exclusive mens' refuge

WHERE: 164 Elmwood Ave.

COST: Free viewing of the exterior

PRO TIP: Get a tour of the Saturn Club; you'll never get into this club.

The alleyway entrance has a wrought iron railing and door, both depicting playing card clubs."The Pack" is also visible on the top half of the gate.

Above: The unassuming home of the Pack. Inset: The alleyway entrance gate with a wrought iron heart and spade. Photos by Elizabeth Licata

who preferred to remain anonymous (of course) wrote to Purdy, noting that some Pack Club parties were "affairs that were entirely unfit for the impressionable or the easily offended."

A MID-CENTURY MODERN MECCA

Looking for Knoll? French Art Deco? Mies van der Rohe?

From Eames chairs with Eiffel Tower bases to a Curtis Jere "Cloud" chrome chandelier to a hand-carved Tiki bar, the treasures to be found in CooCooU Modern's vast warehouse of vintage furniture and decor are such that collectors travel from all over the world to search through them. Owner Michael Merisola started amassing mid-century masterpieces decades ago, when many considered them little better than trash. Locals who have never visited the store leave shaking their heads in disbelief and wonder. Here is a place where it's possible to buy pieces now enshrined in design museums and textbooks.

From Wes Anderson–inspired gingerbread houses to dining room sets to retro roadsters, the clean look of mid-century modern has captured the fancies of a minimalist generation. Despite Buffalo's largely Victorian residential architecture, hipsters yearning to live an Instagram-friendly life are finding a way to transform their living spaces, thanks to CooCooU.

COOCOOU MODERN

WHAT: Buffalo's shrine to retro design

WHERE: 111 Tonawanda St.

COST: Free to browse

PRO TIP: If you wait to see pieces displayed on Instagram, it's too late.

"Most of the really, really good shopping happens in Michigan and Buffalo."—Guillermo del Toro's set decorator, Shane Vieau

Some of the eclectic vintage furniture and decor at CooCooU Modern. Photos by Elizabeth Licata

FERMENTED AND FABULOUS

Does it matter that it's good for you?

A 200-acre farm in East Otto, New York, where cows graze freely on grasses and wildflowers, is where it all starts. The yogurt, milk, and dairy tonics that result are among the best to be found in the Northeast. Sold under the label White Cow Dairy, the dairy items are joined by homemade granolas, jams, soups, and baked goods from local artisans in a tiny Buffalo storefront called the Farm Shop. The shop was founded by Patrick Lango, an enthusiastic dairy farmer who decided to make yogurt from his high-quality milk.

In an interview for *Edible Buffalo*, Lango states, "When people ask me why [my product] tastes so good, the answer is, I do as little as possible. This process is really about bringing out the character of the milk. If you start with great milk; you'll get a great food. That is—if you don't mess with it." Lango first sold his yogurt wholesale, to great acclaim, but found he would do better with his own year-round shop. It's Buffalo's gain.

FARM SHOP

WHAT: A small shop featuring dairy products that are just about perfect

WHERE: 241 Lexington Ave.

COST: Yogurts start at $3.

PRO TIP: Watch the store's Facebook page for specials and pop-ups.

Before establishing in Buffalo, White Cow Dairy sold its yogurt at Murray's Cheese and other Manhattan outlets to rave reviews.

Above: White Cow sells Fresh dairy and homemade goods from local artisans. Photo by kc kratt photography. Inset: Chilled White Cow yogurt. Photo courtesy of White Cow

One of White Cow's early investors was actress Rene Russo, who enthused in an 2014 interview with a San Francisco paper, "It started and we've gotten amazing write-ups as the best yogurt in the country. It's called White Cow Dairy. Whole Foods [grocery store] said they wanted us, but we didn't want to go because we wanted to keep it local sustainable foods for the farmers because they're paying nothing. It's helpful to the community, and it's really healthy. I thought this would be fun to do, and we have one store [in Buffalo]. So we'll see where it goes."

NICHE, OBSCURE, AND COOL

Looking for the perfect pennant?

Entrepreneurs Dave Horesh and Brett Mikoll found that if they wanted pennants with the retro designs they were looking for, they'd have to make them themselves, so they started a company that specializes in custom wool felt pennants, emblazoned with a wide variety of logos, sayings, and imagery. At first, their sales were online or through pop-ups, but they established a permanent retail presence in 2018.

The store also carries T-shirts, hoodies, mugs, and socks, as well as merchandise from other companies. Oxford Pennant has a unique presence in Buffalo: it roots for Buffalo teams, combats the COVID-19 doldrums with heartening banners, and runs myriad promotions and contests to keep things interesting. One of the most famous of these was its contest awarding the winner a free trip to Buffalo during February. The first pennant Horesh and Mikoll produced was, "Let's Go, Buffalo!" Now, clients include Adidas, Facebook, Google, Burton, WordPress, and Yahoo.

OXFORD PENNANT

WHAT: Cool pennants for New Buffalo and beyond

WHERE: 731 Main St.

COST: Pennants start at $25

PRO TIP: One of the most popular pennants is, "Keep Buffalo a Secret."

"Just walking into the place is a mood-enhancing experience—a jumbo-sized pennant on the wall reads, 'It's good to have you with us even if it's just for the day.'"—*Atlas Obscura*

Custom pennants and other gear by Oxford Pennant. Photos courtesy of Oxford Pennant

Looking for a pennant? Thought you knew what pennants were all about? Think again. Oxford Pennant offers a series of custom victory banners for the Buffalo Bills football team (one shown here), custom Christmas stockings, pandemic-friendly safety signage, and even—once—a free trip to Buffalo during winter. Here's a company that lives by creative thinking.

SOCIAL JUSTICE IN ACTION

Can weaving, sewing, and knitting help bring peace and community?

In a modest storefront on Buffalo's West Side, a thriving community of more than 55 women from Bhutan, Burma, Nepal, Thailand, and Angola come together weekly to form a Refugee Women's Workshop, sewing handcrafted goods for sale within the community.

Director Dawne Hoeg began the organization as a series of sewing workshops, which became so popular that she decided to form a nonprofit that would help Buffalo's refugee women learn skills or use their existing skills to help them earn money and make connections with the local community.

The women make and sell their work in the Stitch Buffalo shop, using donated materials. They also take commissions for special orders. Recently, Stitch Buffalo has been creating a series of small, colorful peace pins, a form of activism in conjunction with Black Lives Matter. It has been selling the pins to help raise funds for such organizations as the Underground Railroad Heritage Center, the International Institute of Buffalo, and the Western New York Peace Center.

Hoeg explained the group's mission in an 2020 interview with Buffalo Rising: "We strive to make everyone feel welcome in our space—and that's especially important for people who may face language and cultural obstacles when settling into their

---

"It's tear-jerking, really, because at every payout, there are always new women who are getting their first paycheck." —Stitch Buffalo founder Dawne Hoeg

Top: Artists collaborating on new pieces. Inset: Stitch Buffalo creations. Photos courtesy of Stitch Buffalo

STITCH BUFFALO

WHAT: An inspirational, needlework-based nonprofit

WHERE: 1215 Niagara St.

COST: Pins are $15–$20; larger, more elaborate items cost more.

PRO TIP: To really get to the heart of this place, take a class.

new communities. One of the key ways we make Stitch Buffalo as open and accessible as possible is by operating on a drop-in basis. Our artists are free to stop in to drop off work or collect supplies whenever we are open. We also welcome them to bring their children or spouses, and to come in groups if that eases transportation issues or feels more comfortable."

BUFFALO'S OTHER LIGHTHOUSE

How has this obscure and inaccessible landmark survived?

The Buffalo Harbor South Entrance Light is also known as the South Buffalo Southside Light, Buffalo South Breakwater, or South Entrance Light Station, but those few Buffalonians who are aware of its existence just call it the South Buffalo Lighthouse. It consists of a three-story, cast-iron, 43-foot decommissioned light tower topped with a lantern; a one-story concrete fog signal building; and an L-shaped, concrete pier. Built in 1904, the lighthouse was decommissioned in 1962, at which point it was left to the elements for almost 50 years. In 2011, it was acquired by the Buffalo Lighthouse Association and currently is being restored. Although it still needs more than $500,000 worth of

SOUTH BUFFALO LIGHTHOUSE

WHAT: Guardian of the south entrance to Buffalo's outer harbor

WHERE: Edge of the old Bethlehem Steel Plant, on private property

COST: The price of a boat ride

PRO TIP: In a few years, there may be easier ways to see this, as Buffalo's harbor continues its redevelopment.

Unlike its handsome counterpart on Fuhrmann Road, the iconic 1833 Buffalo Lighthouse, the South Buffalo Light rarely is visited. One reason for this is that it must be reached by boat; it is bordered by privately owned industrial property.

South Buffalo lighthouse. Photo courtesy of the US Coast Guard

work, the structure looks much better and has acquired some protective steel fencing to secure it from further storm damage. Eventually, the plan is to restore it fully and include a new light, docks, an interactive museum, and more. In the meantime, it's worth a scenic boat ride across the Buffalo harbor to view this tough survivor of Lake Erie's winter fury.

The station was deeded to the Buffalo Lighthouse Association in 2012, under the National Historic Lighthouse Preservation Act. An $850,000 project is planned to restore the station and reuse it for maritime education in partnership with the M.A.I.N. Foundation, as a shoreline study center and as a site for amateur radio activities.

EVERY PAPER HAS A STORY

Have you ever considered expressing yourself with wallpaper?

Red Disk started as a way to bring artist Charles Burchfield's 1920s-era wallpaper designs for Buffalo's M. H. Birge & Sons Company back to life—in partnership with the Burchfield Penney Art Center—and make them available in the marketplace. This mission has been expanded greatly. The company works with local artists, who create designs that are then silkscreened and printed to order. For many Buffalonians, the idea of filling their rooms with the original designs of Buffalo's most well-known artist must be irresistible. Burchfield spent only eight years at Birge—it was a way to support his family before his art career took off—but it's easy to see why he quickly became head of the design department. Even in wallpaper, Burchfield's use of abstracted natural forms and his own language of symbolic imagery is apparent immediately in compelling, beautiful designs.

RED DISK

WHAT: A personal wallpaper company

WHERE: Check reddiskstudio.com for locations

COST: Varies

PRO TIP: The Burchfield papers are probably the best choices for Victorian or Arts & Crafts homes.

Red Disk soon moved on to add contemporary artists to its repertoire. One of them is Jozef Bajus, an award-winning

"The artist is a partner with us . . . and so we translate their work, their artwork to wallpaper so they're all original artists' designs." —Red Disk cofounder Tracy Ackerman

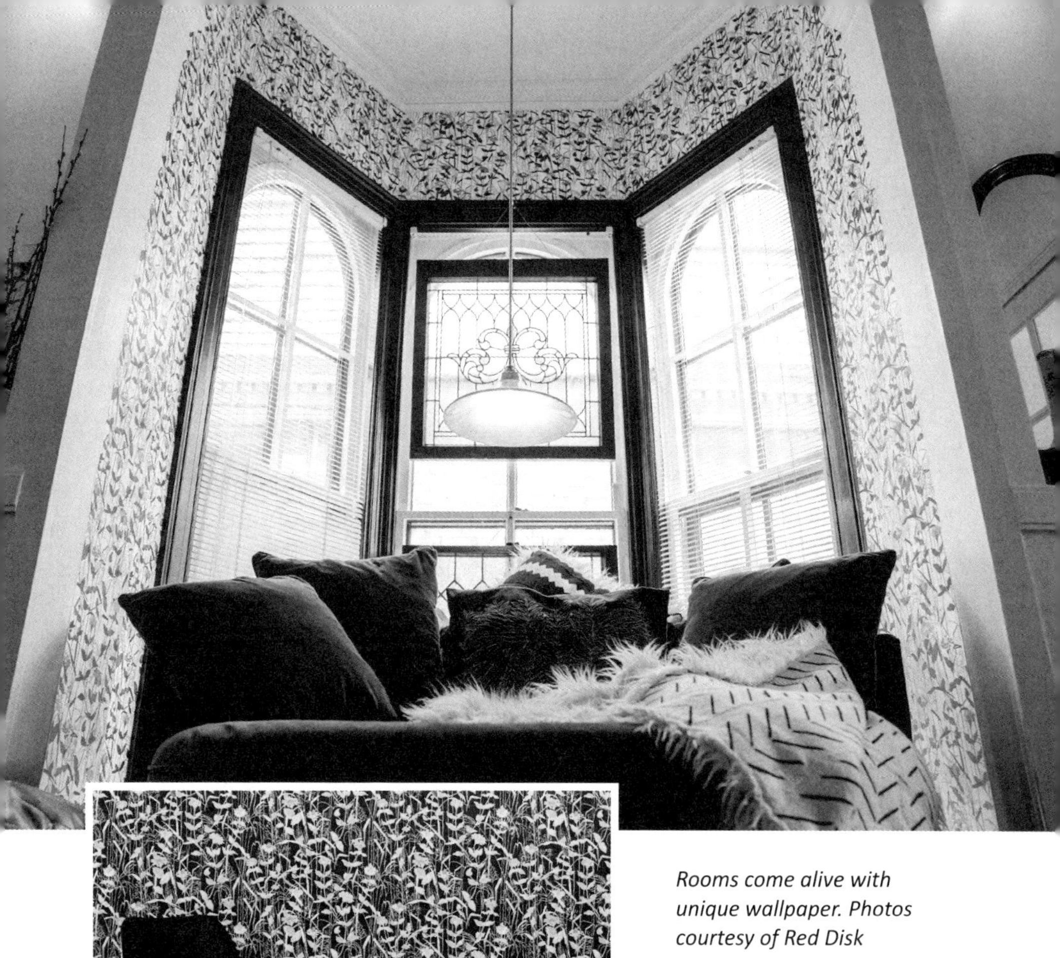

Rooms come alive with unique wallpaper. Photos courtesy of Red Disk

mixed-media artist and sculptor who works extensively with fibers and assorted recycled materials. His use of repurposed materials connects to his overarching theme of understanding the environment and society's impact on it. The composition of his pieces displays complex relationships between these materials, and subsequently causes viewers to reflect on their own complex relationships with them. Imagine having such an artist creating the papers for the walls that surround you.

A LATE SUMMER DESTINATION

Is it possible to have too many flowers?

In 2016, local farmers Chad and Louise Danielewicz decided to open their field of sunflowers, which they had planted as a cover crop, to the public. The field immediately became the subject matter of hundreds of Instagram and Facebook posts (often sunflower selfies). Eventually, the Danielewiczes created amenities for visitors, including a capacious parking lot, a refreshment stand, a gift shop, a gem mine, and seating. Yoga classes and cosplayers have enlivened the scene, and there is even a "U-Pick" option. Visitors are reported from all over the Northeast and Midwest. Comments on the site's Facebook page tell inspirational stories of how the fields of flowers stirred memories of loved ones and motivated acts of kindness. While sunflowers are grown everywhere, either in gardens or commercially for their seeds, it's not often that it's possible to wander through a huge field of sunflowers without trespassing.

SUNFLOWERS OF SANBORN

WHAT: A huge field of sunflowers open to the public

WHERE: 3311 Saunders Settlement Rd., Sanborn, NY

COST: $20 and up, depending on concessions and other extras

PRO TIP: Try this popular destination on weekdays to beat the crowds.

Get lost in a field of sunflowers.
Photos by Elizabeth Licata

"I don't think there's anything on this planet that more trumpets life than the sunflower. . . . Wherever light is, no matter how weak, these flowers will find it. And that's such an admirable thing. And such a lesson in life."
—Helen Mirren as Chris in *Calendar Girls*

IN THE SHADOW OF THE SILOS

Can industry and art collaborate?

There is something about proximity to the grain elevators—interior or exterior—that sharpens the senses and stimulates the imagination. No matter what is being heard or seen, it is more exciting to see it inside one of these concrete giants—or maybe just outside, with the Buffalo River as an additional scenic backdrop.

As one example, for the past seven years, Just Buffalo Literary Center has held poetry readings, art installations, and musical performances at Silo City. Each of the scheduled dates features readings by two poets, one local, one visiting; some sort of installation or other creation from a visual artist; and music. According to Just Buffalo, the participating artists are just as much in awe of the experience as the audience: "Reading poems in a grain elevator while rain fell outside was one of the most amazing poetry experiences I've ever had," says writer Maggie Smith.

SILO CITY READING SERIES

WHAT: Summer evenings of poetry and more

WHERE: Silo City, 92 Child St.

COST: Free

PRO TIP: Stop by Duende, which has a spacious backyard, for drinks and food.

"The Silo City Reading Series is magical," says poet Mathias Svalina. "It drops the artists and audience into a nexus of history, commerce, nature's reclamations, and the radical work of imagination."

Top: Industry and the arts combine at Silo City. Photo by Elizabeth Licata. Inset: Silo City poster. Photo courtesy of Just Buffalo

Thanks to Buffalo businessman Rick Smith, who created Silo City, these formerly abandoned and somewhat scary structures have become places of art, literature, music, and dance. They have become places to gather, eat, drink, and celebrate. Smith is the owner of nearby Rigidized Metals Corporation on Ohio Street, a company founded by Rick's grandfather, Rick "Stainless" Smith, in 1938. Smith, and others, are helping the grain elevators evolve from abandoned monoliths to places of art to a neighborhood where people can live, work, and play year-round.

BUFFALO'S OLDEST GAY BAR

Why is a place like this essential?

Underground Niteclub has existed under various names since 1974. It literally is underground, down a flight of stairs below a handsome apartment building on Delaware Avenue in downtown Buffalo. Long accepted as an old-school hangout for Buffalo's LGBTQ community, the bar is welcoming and understated. Nobody knew how beloved it was until it was threatened with closure in 2018.

UNDERGROUND NITECLUB

WHAT: One of Buffalo's oldest LGBTQ watering holes

WHERE: 274 Delaware Ave.

COST: Price of a drink and occasional covers for special events

PRO TIP: Be cool.

The official reason was that its building was under US Department of Housing and Urban Development (HUD) ownership, and HUD had received complaints from the tenants of the subsidized apartments above the bar. Everything was ironed out, eventually, and the bar reopened, to much relief and jubilation from the community. Even better, the management took advantage of the brief hiatus to refresh some of the seen-better-days interior decor.

In an era where same-sex marriage is legal, and LGBTQ men and women are overcoming all odds to be elected to national political office, gay bars may seem trivial, but they remain important waystations for empowerment.

This innocuous entrance leads to one of Buffalo's oldest LGBTQ clubs. Photo by Elizabeth Licata

Owner/manager Nick Tiede expressed relief and stressed the importance of the club's presence in an interview with the *Buffalo News*: "I think it's great that we can maintain one of our safe spaces for the LGBT community. Underground gets a diverse crowd so it's a place for people to feel comfortable and call home. I think it's keeping a piece of our history alive, and it's also an opportunity for our community's future."

BIZARRE INTERSECTIONS

Ever wonder why getting around Buffalo can be so strangely confusing?

Some would say it's all about the intersections. Proceeding through some of them is like a multiple-choice quiz—with at least six possible answers—that has to be answered correctly in four seconds. Why are there so many parallel roads feet from each other, with multiple stop signs, at Forest Avenue and Lincoln Parkway? Who created the nightmare at Main, Goodell, Pearl, and Edward? Ever notice how easy it is to go the wrong way down Humboldt Parkway? We won't even get into the circles.

Peter Gorman, a Syracuse-born artist who graduated from the University at Buffalo, took an 11,000-mile bike ride across the US that inspired a series of minimalist designs based on urban geography. The projects include the Manhattan subway system, the parks of Savannah, and a series of "Intersections," which depict crazy intersections in Houston, Pittsburgh, Chicago, Austin, and, of course, Buffalo. Gorman's Barely Maps project can be found on Etsy.

INTERSECTIONS OF BUFFALO

WHAT: Graphic depictions of odd intersections

WHERE: Etsy/Intersections of Buffalo

COST: Starting at $27

PRO TIP: Avoid Main, Pearl, Edward, and Goodell at all costs.

Buffalonians really have little to complain about when it comes to traffic. The average work commute in Buffalo is never more than half an hour and usually much less.

Buffalo's intersections. Photo courtesy of barelymaps

There's now a book by Gorman entitled *Barely Maps*. As Gorman describes it, "Originally inspired by a one-year, 11,000-mile, solo bicycle trip around the US and Canada, *Barely Maps* is a collection of 100 minimalist maps. It's also a story about the bike trip, the designs themselves, and all of the other stuff—before and after."

WOMEN OF THE PEN

Will there always be a place for poets?

In 2016, the oldest feminist literary periodical in the US celebrated its 45th anniversary. Called *Earth's Daughters*, it was founded in Buffalo by poet Judith Kerman and currently is edited by Kastle Brill, Jennifer Campbell, Joan Ford, Joyce Kessel, Janna Willoughby-Lohr, and ryki zuckerman. The publication has survived.

In 1971, Kerman was attending poetry readings and reading literary journals in Buffalo, noting that few featured work by women. Kerman wanted a place "where the welcome for women was unequivocal." She founded a new magazine, its name inspired by Emma Goldman's *Mother Earth.*

Founder Kerman credits the journal's survival to the fact that *Earth's Daughters* has a hardworking and dedicated group of women deeply committed to its success and that it publishes poetry and prose that people can read and enjoy. "You shouldn't have to have a PhD to enjoy poetry," she notes. The Earth's Daughters team does not want the magazine to forsake print and paper; they feel that editing a paper copy is more reliable and accurate than editing online and that there is great pleasure in "passing things back and forth" between readers.

EARTH'S DAUGHTERS

WHAT: Feminist literary and arts periodical

WHERE: Earthsdaughters.org for subscriptions

COST: $27

PRO TIP: Look for the back issues, many of which are in unusual formats.

Left: Earth's Daughters' *coeditor ryki zuckerman. Photo by kc kratt photography.*
Right: Earth's Daughters' *coeditor Kastle Brill. Photo by kc kratt photography*

The Key
Is solid
And fits well in
The palm of
Your hand.

It is for
The door
At the end of
The hall

And slides into
The lock
With a turning
Click.

—(excerpt) Tennise Morse,
from first issue of *Earth's Daughters*, 1971

THE CHURCH THAT BECAME A LIVING SCULPTURE

Is it possible to reclaim a lost art?

In 2014, artist Dennis Maher purchased the former Immaculate Conception Church at 150 Edward St., where it meets Elmwood. After three years of stabilizing the structure and adapting the interior for his purposes, Maher unveiled the Assembly House 150 building as a project space and training center. Called the Society for the Advancement of Construction-Related Arts (SACRA), Maher's training program is undertaken in collaboration with the Albright-Knox Art Gallery, Buffalo Public Schools, and the Erie County Department of Social Services. Through this program, adult students will learn skills they need for employment—such as carpentry and woodworking—and, even more important, learn to use their imaginations to solve interesting problems. The space is lined with ornate, mixed-media constructions. At its

ASSEMBLY HOUSE 150

WHAT: A creative training program, combining art, design, and construction

WHERE: 150 Edward St.

COST: Free, but contact them first.

PRO TIP: This structure is near an intersection with several other distinctive historic buildings, including St. Mary's Condominiums, the Mansion on Delaware Avenue, and the Buffalo Club.

"These days everyone watches YouTube videos to learn how to construct things. We use beautiful instruction manuals."—Dennis Maher, Assembly House 150

Top: A repurposed church brings new developments. Photo by David Schalliol; inset photo by Dennis Maher

core in the former church transept is a monumental, black, hollow sculpture, big enough to hold rooms where classes could be taught and workshops held. Check the website for information on the program: assemblyhouse150.org.

Some of the projects that Maher and his students have undertaken include a porch on Normal Avenue, a mobile children's library set up in an old camper, a decorative pattern wall mural at a local workforce training center, and more. Most of the students who have completed the program have since been placed in area firms.

A SECRET STREET

Where can you find a tiny English village in the middle of the city?

In 1928, Edward B. Green Sr. and Edward B. Green Jr., along with Albert Hart Hopkins, designed Mayfair Lane. This father-and-son architectural team is responsible for designing many of Buffalo's most distinctive structures. The lane's unique driveway-style entrance gives no clue to what lies above—fanciful private Tudor-style townhouses with a castle at the end of the double row of houses. As pedestrians and drivers pass by, Mayfair Lane appears to be a carport and nothing more. Mayfair Lane was designed to solve the problem of those who want to live in the city but prefer a secluded, village-like neighborhood. The Mayfair Lane community remains intact more than 80 years after it was originally constructed.

Mayfair Lane has not been without its controversies. A recent purchaser of the "castle"

MAYFAIR LANE

WHAT: A charming small enclave in the middle of Allentown

WHERE: Off Allen Street, across from Allen and Irving Place

COST: Free

PRO TIP: You can only glimpse the lane from the street or sidewalk; it is private.

It's a simple idea, really. The vehicular lane is at ground level, and a pedestrian lane is built above. You pull in and park under your unit. Guests parking on the street walk up two stairways either side of the vehicular entry to the pedestrian lane. —Steve Mouzon, Studiosky.co

An English village in Allentown. Photos by Jim Bush

at the end of the lane put up a gate that immediately evoked outrage from his neighbors. The gate remains; it was denied by the tenant association but approved by the city's preservation board. There is a governing board of its property owners; in addition, the structures are subject to historic preservation guidelines. Changes to the structures cannot be undertaken without a series of permits. Nonetheless, this charming, under-the-radar street contains some of Buffalo's most coveted properties.

A REVITALIZED INDUSTRIAL HISTORY SITE

How does an "infected district" reinvent itself to offer a healthier type of entertainment?

While the battle for the rewatering of the Erie Canal terminus is well remembered by most in Buffalo—nearly everyone has seen the ice skating in winter and paddleboating in summer—an adjacent micro-neighborhood, forming a bond between Canalside and the beginnings of South Buffalo and the grain elevator district, is less known. Most first-time visitors to the breweries, distilleries, and nightclubs located here go through brief head-scratching moments before figuring out the right turns to take. Yet, this is one of those most credible elements of an area whose

COBBLESTONE DISTRICT

WHAT: A waterfront enclave of entertainment, residential, and offices areas

WHERE: Bounded by Perry, Illinois, and Columbia Streets and South Park Avenue

COST: Depends on which venue you patronize

PRO TIP: The Helium Comedy Club, Buffalo Iron Works, and Lockhouse Distillery all provide nationally recognized acts and products.

The battle for the Erie Canal Harbor historic/recreation/commercial site is well underway, and we are winning. This thing remains a work in progress. The icing needs fixing. But we have baked a pretty good cake.
—Donn Esmond, *Buffalo News*, 2008

Cobblestone District murals. Photo courtesy of Albright Knox

original 19th-century commercial roots are long forgotten. First, there are the cobbles lining the short streets named after states. Then there are the industrial characters of nearly all the structures and interiors, whether truly authentic or determinedly so. There's plenty to do here, along with some great walks in any season.

Distinctive buildings include Buffalo Iron Works at 49 Illinois St. The restored 1915 industrial structure features brick walls, tall ceilings, exposed air ducts, and salvaged architectural relics. And don't forget, just steps away, is Canalside proper, another previously forgotten and neglected area that is now a popular destination in all seasons. It is anchored by a piece of art that nobody fails to visit: *Shark Girl*, by artist Casey Riordan Millard.

The small district is not without its complications. Larger waterfront development projects could envelop some of the older structures that have not yet been renovated. In a 2020 *Buffalo News* article, Jessie Fisher, executive director of Preservation Buffalo Niagara noted, "This tiny block of the Cobblestone District represents, really, the last intact part of our waterfront related to the Erie Canal. This is our last connection to that part of our heritage."

A SUPERB CATHEDRAL TO ARTS AND CRAFTS

Where can you find 50,000 of the highest-quality art products anywhere?

Hyatt's, the largest art store in the US, was founded in Buffalo 50 years ago, and while many locals think of it as a nice, neighborhood place to get some arts supplies, artists know better. They know there are only a handful of stores throughout the US that offer this many diverse art supplies at such a high professional level. But there are others besides artists who depend on Hyatt's. The store supplies brands such as Adidas, Asics, and Eddie Bauer with Pantone products for color matching. It provides highway and public works departments with street signage design and printing. Hyatt's also has wonderful coloring books and crayons and offers classes.

HYATT'S

WHAT: A cornucopia of art supplies

WHERE: 1941 Elmwood Ave.

COST: It depends on what you need.

PRO TIP: The Pantone-branded items make great gifts.

"We ship out anywhere between 400 to 600 packages each day. About 150 of those are outside of the United States."
—Seth Martin, purchasing director of Hyatt's All Things Creative.

Art supplies and so much more.
Photos by Stephen Gabris

It has always been the go-to for Sunday painters, art students, and teachers seeking supplies. Most of these customers browsing its former location on Main Street downtown likely had no idea that more than 50 workers behind the scenes were involved in shipping, receiving, creating vinyl wraps and commercial signage, and making custom frames.

With a new, larger facility, Hyatt's can still fulfill the needs of its local clientele as well as maintain its international business profile.

A WATER TOWER PAINTED LIKE A SANDWICH

Will it happen?

In late 2018, a design competition was held to determine a possible design to paint a blue water tower in Hamburg, just south of Buffalo, so that the tower would resemble an actual hamburger. The thinking behind this is that the 1885 Erie County Fair, held in Hamburg, saw the birth of the first US hamburger. The winner of this competition, determined by a vote among Hamburg residents, was graphic designer Dylan Cownie, a Tonawanda resident.

However, months after Cownie was chosen, the design has not yet been implemented. There is now a Hamburger Water Tower Trust, set up for the purposes of raising funds so that the prizewinning design may become reality.

It must be said that there is still some debate about Hamburg as the true birthplace of the hamburger. There are several other contenders, including Athens, Texas; Seymour, Wisconsin; and New Haven, Connecticut.

HAMBURGER TOWER

WHAT: A municipal water tower that salutes its supposed namesake

WHERE: Hamburg

COST: Free

PRO TIP: This may or may not actually be completed.

"We want them to have a reason to come to the Southtowns. We think painting the water tower will really help us stand out," Luly said, adding, "If we paint it, they will come."
—Chris Hannotte Luly, *Buffalo News*, 2019

Hamburg Water Tower - design by Dylan Cownie

Top: Future plans for the water tower. Inset: Prizewinning designer Dylan Cownie (left) next to his design. Photos courtesy of Dylan Cownie

According to local historian Steve Cichon, the problem with the Erie County Fair story is that the Menches, the vendors who presumably served it in Hamburg in 1885, took decades to tell the story of their invention to anyone and also claimed to have invented it at an Ohio fair. The Erie County Fair origin claim did not really become widely known until the 1980s. As Cichon notes, it's a fun story.

AN ELEGANT WOMEN'S CLUB

How did women get out of the house in 1894?

Founded by teacher and civic organizer Charlotte Mulligan, Buffalo's Twentieth Century Club is now more than 125 years old. Its orginal purpose was to advance the interests of education, literature, and art. The current headquarters was finished in 1896 and designed as a clubhouse, with further additions in 1905. Designed in the Italian Renaissance style, the imposing structure is the location for weekly meetings of its members, which include lectures by local political leaders, artists, and influencers from all walks of life; a lunch; and a social hour. Its members are always working behind the scenes to organize events and trips, maintain the historic structure, take care of the beautiful Italian-style garden, and much more. The club is the site of weddings, celebrations, and events of all types; all who enter it for the first time are impressed by its lavish interior, which includes two galleries, a paneled library, a ballroom, a music room

TWENTIETH CENTURY CLUB

WHAT: A private women's club that's available for events, within limits

WHERE: 595 Delaware Ave.

COST: Free with an invitation to an event or with the cost of a membership

PRO TIP: Contact the Club for public tours of this lovely National Landmark.

While many private clubs are thought of as elite bastions of privilege, most members here are retired teachers or other retired members of various occupations who are finally taking the time to learn more about the region and relax with friends.

Left: The court, featuring a sculpted frieze. Right: Exterior of building with garden. Photos by kc kratt photography

with original murals, and a court ornamented by a sculpted frieze based on Luca Della Robbia's *Cantoria*. The Court is a large central room, square in shape, elegant in proportion. Its high traditional ceiling is punctuated with leaded-glass skylights, and the room is ringed with ionic columns, its symmetrical openings arranged in a beautiful rhythm. It serves as an elegant organizing space, around which the entire floorplan circulates. Two grand marble staircases with elaborate bronze balustrades ascend to the second (and principal) floor. All this grandeur is virtually unknown to most Buffalonians, unless they have been invited to a wedding or other event. For the most part, the club is inhabited by its hardworking members, who are dedicated to their mission of keeping the club vibrant and available for future generations of Western New York women.

ANOTHER BELOVED DOG

How did Greek restaurateurs come up with a Texas hot?

"Whether you call it a slime dog, scum dog or 'some kind' of a canoe, the 'Texas hot' is a Western New York institution and one of those tastes you just can't find outside of the 716."—Steve Cichon, *Buffalo News*, 11/9/20

According to longtime Western New York chef/ photographer Joe George, Texas Red Hots are "pure Buffalo. There seems to be nothing actually 'Texan' about Texas hots, other than that the sauce somewhat resembles chili con carne in appearance, not flavor. The culinary historian in me says that the sauce actually has more in common with ancient Greek or Roman cooking than it does Texas [the meat is not sautéed or fried, it's boiled with spices and thickened with breadcrumbs instead]. One story I had come across some time ago is that they were first concocted at a downtown Greek diner that was located opposite a Deco restaurant. At the time, Deco was offering a 25-cent wiener-and-beans dinner that was luring customers away from the diner. In order to stay competitive, the diner owner offered a hot dog special with his secret sauce on it and called it a Texas Red Hot after its resemblance to chili."

Many Buffalonians agree with George that a Texas Red Hot is all about the sauce. George's recipe is included here.

TEXAS RED HOTS

WHAT: Another, lesser-known Buffalo fast-food specialty

WHERE: Louie's Texas Red Hots, 7 locations; Seneca Texas Hots, 2449 Seneca St.; Zorba's Texas Hots, 6184 Transit Rd., Depew

COST: $3-$10, depending on how many dogs

PRO TIP: Don't expect anything Texan about these; just order two to get the full experience.

Texas Red Hot Sauce
(recipe by Joe George, as published in *Buffalo Spree*, 4/07)
Prep time: 2 and 1/2 hours
Number of servings: makes 3 quarts

Ingredients:

- 3 tablespoons vegetable oil
- 3 cups minced onions
- 2 tablespoons minced garlic
- 2 quarts water
- 2 pounds ground beef
- 1/2 cup chili powder
- 1/3 cup paprika
- 2 tablespoons ground cumin
- 2 tablespoons ground cinnamon
- 2 tablespoons oregano
- 1 tablespoon ground allspice
- 1 tablespoon salt
- 2 teaspoons dry mustard
- 1 teaspoon cayenne pepper
- 1 teaspoon ground black pepper
- 1-1/2 cups unseasoned breadcrumbs
- 1-2 teaspoons Tabasco sauce (optional)

Directions:
Combine the oil, onions, and garlic in a heavy-bottomed saucepot, and cook over medium heat for 15 minutes or until dark golden brown. Stir often to avoid scorching. Add the water and bring to a boil. Add the beef and stir to break apart any lumps of meat. Return the sauce to a boil, and stir in the chili powder, paprika, cumin, cinnamon, oregano, allspice, salt, mustard, cayenne pepper, and black pepper; stir to remove any lumps. Lower the heat to a low simmer, and cook the sauce for 1 hour, stirring frequently and skimming off any excess fat (there will be a fair amount of fat from the beef). Stir in the breadcrumbs, and simmer over low heat for 30-60 minutes. Stir the sauce frequently to avoid scorching. If the sauce is not thick enough for your liking, add more breadcrumbs; if it is too thick, dilute it with water.

NATURE BATS LAST

Is Buffalo best in winter?

Even a non-skiing Buffalonian has plenty of options in winter. Six Audubon Society sites hug the southeastern edges of Western New York. The main site, Beaver Meadow, is in the wonderfully named North Java (pronounced JAY-vuh). It has a visitor's center that is lined with windows in the back, all the better to catch the action around a large group of feeders. Beyond the feeders are wooded trails around a large pond. Watch the birds from inside, or go outside and hang quietly. Then, take a walk around the pond and take in the undeniable beauty of the winter landscape.

BUFFALO IN WINTER

WHAT: Embracing the cold months

WHERE: Throughout the region

COST: Free

PRO TIP: Bundle up and get out there.

Steady, the evening fades
up the street into sunset
over the lake. Winter sits
quiet here, snow piled
by the road, the walks stamped
down or shoveled. The kids
in the time before dinner are
playing, sliding on the old ice.
The dogs are out, walking.
And it's soon inside again,
with the light gone.
Time to eat, to think of it all.
—"Buffalo Evening" by Robert Creeley

Top: Beaver Meadow. Inset: Buffalonians enjoying winter. Photos by Elizabeth Licata

Beaver Meadow has 324 acres of marked trails, glacial kettle ponds, a boardwalk trail, and an arboretum. Although it's visited less than many preserves closer to the city, Beaver Meadow offers more of a bird focus and better interpretive information than many.

Other winter go-tos here are Reinstein Woods Nature Preserve, a refuge for wildlife and native plants surrounded by suburban developments, and Tifft Nature Preserve, which is designated an Important Bird Area. Throughout winter, even amateurs can easily spot cardinals, blue jays, goldfinches, downy and red-bellied woodpeckers, chickadees, and junkos. If adequately clothed (and maybe equipped with a pair of snowshoes), one may find a sense of quiet adventure on winter walks.

SOURCES

Art Underground: Buffalo as an Architectural Museum: Metro Rail Stations (buffaloah.com/a/metro/tc.html).

The House That a Prophecy Built: roadsideamerica.com/story/38832.

Priceless Library Treasures: buffalolib.org/special-collections/rare-book-room.

An Old-School IMAX: Healey, Meg. "The Cyclorama Building," Buffalo as an Architectural Museum (buffaloah.com/a/franklin/369/).

Second Life for a Demolished Landmark: Multiple authors. *Buffalo Architecture: A Guide*. MIT Press, 1981.

Spooky Magnificence in Perrysburg: Licata, Elizabeth. "J. N. Adam Memorial Hospital," *Buffalo Spree* magazine, December, 2010.

A Visit to an Old Flame: Kershner, Bruce. *Secret Places*, Kendall Hunt Publishing, 1994.

A Dream of a Western New York Jewish Homeland: Chana Revell Kotzin, *Jewish Community of Greater Buffalo*; Canfield, Michael. *Buffalo News*, April 6, 2016.

Underground Railroad History in Western New York: niagarafallsundergroundrailroad.org

Buffalo's Barbary Coast: Vogel, Michael. *America's Crossroads*. Heritage Press, 1993.

From Perilous Shantytown to Peaceful Preserve: Bohen, Timothy. *Against the Grain*, 2012; friendsoftimesbeachnp.org.

Stones of a Little-Known History: Revell Kotzin, Chana. *Jewish Community of Greater Buffalo*. Arcadia Publishing, 2013.

A Multipurpose Historic Center: polishcadetsofbuffalo.com.

Hike the Ravines: https://www2.erie.gov/parks/index.php?q=franklin-gulf-0.

A Refuge for Rare Waterfowl: Rising, Gerry. "Goose Hill," *Buffalo Spree*, August 2019.

A Culinary Legend: Seychew, Christa. "At The Table: Buffalo's Stuffed Peppers, New and Old," *Buffalo Spree*, March 2016.

The Court with the Mostest: Interview with Nick Vitello, October 2000; imperialcourtofbuffalo.com.

A Creek Runs through It: albertorey. com/s-a-r-e-p-youth-fly-fishing-program/history-of-canadaway-creek.

Another Great Escape: niagaracounty.com/parks/Royalton-Ravine-Park.

The Gorge Is the Thing: Swearingen, Wendy. *Buffalo Spree*, "Hiking the gorge," September 2016.

The Mighty Zoar: Kershner, Bruce. *Secret Places*, Kendall Hunt Publishing, 1994.

This Is Only a Test: Interview with Stan Swisher, June 2020.

Look Up: Interior-Rotunda, Buffalo Savings Bank/Goldome (buffaloah.com).

The Wildest City Hall in the US: Conlin, John. *Buffalo City Hall*. Landmark Society, 1993.

Buffalo is Full of It: Bovino, Arthur. *Buffalo Everything*. The Countryman Press, 2018.

Guarded by a Mountain Lion: Bemis/Ransom House (buffaloah.com).

A High School Gymnasium Loaded with History: Kirst, Sean. *Buffalo News*, June 4, 2017.

A Secluded Shoreline Spot: exploringniagara.com.

Get on the Bus: Nyhuis, Philip. "Exploring Buffalo history through neighborhood taverns," *Buffalo Spree*, October 2009.

The Bar with No Stools: Ohler, Rick. "Wallenwein's," *Buffalo Spree*, February 2016.

Glory to the Heroes: ukrainiansofbuffalo.com.

Where to Watch a Sunset: Licata, Elizabeth. *Buffalo Spree*, July 2018.

Not Just Another Dive: Oswald, Vanessa. *The Public*, February 7, 2018.

A Three-Story Paradise for Readers: Neville, Anne. *Buffalo News*, August 23, 2017.

Life Underground: lockportcave.com/history.

A Magical Backroom: Ali, Sara. "The Tabernacle at Sweet_ness 7 Café" (buffalorising.com).

Mourn a Lost Masterpiece: Williams, James. "An Infamous Demolition," *Buffalo Spree*, July 8, 2006.

Buffalo and the Mob: Hudson, Mike. *Mob Boss*. Power City Press, 2008.

We Don't Say "Buffalo Wings" Here: Bovino, Arthur. *Buffalo Everything*. The Countryman Press, 2018.

A Mental Hospital That Became a Destination: richardson-olmsted.com.

A Tucked-Away Museum: Nyhuis, Philip. "A museum of Larkin Memorabilia," *Buffalo Spree*, November 2019.

The Other St. Patrick's Day Parade: Short, Natalie. "The Old Neighborhood Parade," *Buffalo Spree*, March 2020.

Polish Pastries: Fix Dominguez, Rachel. "What We Want: Paczki," *Buffalo Spree*, February 2012.

A Tiny Secret Garden: Interview with Arlan Peters, May 2006.

A Spectacular Creekside Retreat: Interview with Kathy and Mike Shadrack, April 2017.

The Shed: artofgardening.org.

A True Tale of 'Weck: Bovino, Arthur. *Buffalo Everything*. The Countryman Press, 2018.

You Love the Architecture; Now Check Out the Flowers: Interview with Mary Roberts, June 2020; martinhouse.org.

A District Named for a Dog Biscuit: Puma, Mike. "Walk the Milk-Bone District this Saturday" (buffalorising.com).

Gardenville Is Real: None.

From Zagreb to Buffalo: forgottenbuffalo.com.

Named after a Poet/Activist: forgottenbuffalo.com.

Where to Find Them All: poloniatrail.com.

A Sub for the Ages: Bovino, Arthur. *Buffalo Everything*. The Countryman Press, 2018.

A Place for Everyone: Licata, Elizabeth. "Cicero J. Hamlin's Descendants," *Buffalo Spree*, 7-8/00.

Hatmaker to Hollywood: Bruce Eaton, "Buffalo's Hollywood Hatmaker," *Buffalo Spree*, January 2014.

The Buffalo Sound: Kelley, Frannie. "Griselda Set Out to Be Your Rapper's Favorite Rappers," NPR, December, 19, 2019.

Where a Tight Ethnic Community Gathered: forgottenbuffalo.com.

Putting the Camp into Campground: Ehmke, Ron. "Jones Pond," *Buffalo Spree*, June 2013.

The Art of Saving Art: Levine, Linda. "The Art Doctors," *Buffalo Spree*, September 10, 2001.

When He Was Just an Editor: Reigstad, Thomas J. *Scribblin' for a Livin'*, Prometheus, 2013.

A Posthumous Structure for the Dead: Muskat, Barry. "The State of Wright: Blue Sky Mausoleum," *Buffalo Spree*, July 2012; blueskymausoleum.com.

A Disco-Era Pioneer Continues to Evolve: litelab.com.

A Last Refuge: Purdy, Kevin. "Leaders of the Pack," *Buffalo Spree*, May 2013.

A Mid-Century Modern Mecca: CooCooU27 Furniture Showroom (buffaloah.com).

Fermented and Fabulous: facebook.com/white.cowdairy/.

Niche, Obscure, and Cool: oxfordpennant.com.

Social Justice in Action: stitchbuffalo.org.

Buffalo's Other Lighthouse: lighthousefriends.com.

Every Paper Has a Story: Licata, Elizabeth. "New Wallpaper Firm Builds on Burchfield's Legacy," *Buffalo Spree*, March 2019; reddiskstudio.com.

A Late Summer Destination: Licata, Elizabeth. "Basking in Summer's Finale," *Buffalo Spree*, October 2018.

In the Shadow of the Silos: Justbuffalo.org.

Buffalo's Oldest Gay Bar: Dabkowski, Colin. "Remembering the Underground, Buffalo's Favorite Gay Dive," *Buffalo News*, June 24, 2018.

Bizarre Intersections: Licata, Elizabeth. "Crossways of Buffalo," *Buffalo Spree*, February 2019.

Women of the Pen: Gold Jennifer, "Earth's Daughters," *Buffalo Spree*, March 2016; earthsdaughters.org.

The Church That Became a Living Sculpture: Licata, Elizabeth, "Assembly House 150: When a Church Becomes a Working Sculpture," *Buffalo Spree*, September 2017; assemblyhouse150.org.

A Secret Street: Fox, Austin. "The Greening of Buffalo: How Architect E. B. Green Shaped the Profile of the City," *Buffalo Spree*, Summer/1980.

A Revitalized Industrial Historic Site: cobblestonedistrict.com.

A Superb Cathedral to Arts and Crafts: hyatts.com

A Water Tower Painted Like a Sandwich: Ziomek, Ashley. "Hamburg Water Tower Gets a Makeover," *Buffalo Spree*, February 2019.

An Elegant Women's Club: Muskat, Barry. "A Twenty-First Century Look at the Twentieth Century Club," *Buffalo Spree*, September 2009.

Another beloved dog: George, Joe. "In Praise of the Slider," *Buffalo Spree*, April 2007; Cichon, Steve, "Slime Dog History: Looking at the Past of Buffalo's Texas Hot," *Buffalo News*, November 9, 2000.

Nature Bats Last: Creeley, Robert. "Buffalo Evening," published in several anthologies, including *Mortals & Immortals: Burchfield Penney Art Center 35 Year Anthology*, 2015, and Robert Creeley, *Mirrors*, New Directions, 1983.

Photo by Elizabeth Licata

INDEX

Photo by Elizabeth Licata